PROPHETIC UTTERANCES

From the Holy Spirit &
Words of Encouragement

VOLUME 1

BERNADETTE SMITH

ISBN 000-0-000000-0-0

Copyright © 2023 by Bernadette Smith

Thrive Publishing

Published by Thrive Publishing
1100 Suite #100 Riverwalk Terrace
Jenks, OK 74037

Printed in the United States of America

Contents

HE IS OUR GOOD SHEPHERD 1

OUR FOUNDATION 9

STAY LASER-FOCUSED 17

THE JOY OF THE LORD IS OUR STRENGTH........................23

THERE IS A MENTAL
WAR GOING ON 27

TRUST 33

TRUTH 37

THANKSGIVING 43

LET US GO OVER TO THE OTHER SIDE................................47

THE RIGHT SIDE 53

VICTORY 57

WE WIN...61

LOOK TO JESUS 65

PRAY THE WORD OF GOD 69

THE LORD IS WITH US 73

INDEPENDENCE DAY..77

GOD IS AT WORK MENDING US 81

OUR PRAYERS HAVE BEEN ANSWERED.............................85

JUNETEENTH..89

GOD IS THE REFUGE OF HIS
PEOPLE AND THE CONQUEROR
OF THE NATIONS...95

WE ARE AT A RED SEA MOMENT..99

MOTHER'S DAY...103

LIFE IS PRECIOUS 109

ALL AUTHORITY 113

DO NOT FEAR...117

WHEN WE GET GOD RIGHT, CULTURE FOLLOWS 121

CHOOSING A LEADER IN ANY AREA OF GOVERNMENT 127

THE LORD IS WITH YOU...135

GIVE THANKS...139

FOCUS ON WHAT UNITES US AND RISE ABOVE WHAT
DIVIDES US...145

ENGAGE..151

KEEP THE FAITH..157

WE ARE NOT WRESTLING WITH FLESH AND BLOOD......161

THIS IS AMERICA-...165

THIS IS HEROISM...165

THE LORD IS OUR LIGHT 169

WISDOM 175

RESURRECTION 181

ALIGNMENT...187

NOW WHAT?...191

STAND...195

CHRISTIANITY IS NOT
A DENOMINATION 199

THE FINGER OF GOD...203

WE ARE FREE 207

INTERCEDE...211

IT IS NOT OVER..215

BENEFIT PACKAGE 219

TAKING THE LIMITS OFF GOD 225

REVIVAL..229

WE WIN..233

PRAYING FOR OUR PRESIDENT............................237

CHOOSE LIFE..241

WAY MAKER..243

TIGHTROPE..249

FAITH IS A REST..253

GOD'S WORD APPLIED
BRINGS POWER..257

WE ARE CONQUERORS......................................261

SEEK GOD..265

IT'S A GREAT DAY..269

INDEPENDENCE DAY..273

WAKE UP..277

ARISE..281

BE BOLD..285

THE COVENANT..289

BE ENCOURAGED..293

LOVE WINS..295

DARKNESS AND GROSS DARKNESS..................301

VACCINATE YOURSELF WITH THE WORD OF GOD..........305

UNIFY AROUND THE TRUTH..............................309

SO MUCH NOISE..315

YOUR PLAN..323

UNMASKED..329

HONOR..333

VINDICATION..339

LET'S PRAY..345

INVOCATION FOR THE NATION 349

THE LORD IS OUR SHEPHERD..353

PRAYER FOR SALVATION...357

PRAYER FOR BAPTISM
OF THE HOLY SPIRIT...358

FOREWORD

I love this book, Bernadette! Thanks for having the courage in both your writings and your voice in the many conferences, gatherings, fellowships, and places of ministry where you speak and have influence. God is using you, and God is going to use this book.

To the reader, you'll be able to discover very quickly that Bernadette has done her homework. On every page, you'll also pick up her concern for all of us, especially here in our country, America, and all free countries.

One of my favorite quotes from this book is, "We are totally STRONGER TOGETHER when we rally around the truth."

Bernadette and her husband Phillip have pastored very successfully here in the state of Michigan, and our state would not be as strong as it is without their church, their ministry, and their voice. When you hear Bernadette speak, you can't help but hear her passion for the truth, her compassion for people, and a mixture of great boldness to confront darkness and great love for our Lord and His Word. You will also witness this coming forth as you read this book.

I am standing with you, Bernadette, and I believe this will change people and adjust their compass for the day ahead.

Job well done!

Mark T. Barclay
PREACHER OF RIGHTEOUSNESS

Endorsements

"Prophetic Utterance is a must read! Bernadette Smith shares profound revelations from her personal walk with The Lord. The power of "Decreeing" a matter from the position of Authority granted by The Lord is presented with new understanding. The "Prophetic Word" is expounded upon with practical insights. Prophetic Utterance is a tremendous reference to add to every believer's personal library."

DR. RICHARD BARTLETT

"I had the pleasure of meeting Bernadette Smith nearly two years ago as General Flynn, Eric Trump & I were taking the ReAwaken America Tour across the country. I found Bernadette to be Christ-focused, persistent and full of good energy that can only be found in people that have invited the Holy Spirit into their life. I highly recommend that you read Bernadette's book so that you can be impacted by her ministry and wisdom!"

CLAY CLARK

(U.S. SBA Entrepreneur of the Year, Host of the ThrivetimeShow.com Podcast, founder of the ReAwaken America Tour, founder of many million-dollar companies, author of many books and my mother's second favorite son.)

"It is in trying times like these that those who unflinchingly speak the truth and walk tall in wisdom silently give others the strength and courage to also be brave and unwavering in their fight for God and country. Bernadette Smith has been not only a constant source of inspiration and a guide on my journey, but when I found myself down or exhausted by the battle her words lifted me up and endlessly encouraged me to strive to be better than I even believed I could be. To have been a student and friend of Bernadette has been nothing short of a divine blessing in my life. I cannot recommend her book more passionately, and as someone who feels that but for the grace of God go I finding her words and wisdom has truly been and continues to be an invaluable gift on my journey."

MEL K

(Host The Mel K Show)

"This book is giving us simple but much needed truths that our generation needs. Those who ignore history tend to repeat its mistakes. And ye shall know the truth, and the truth shall make you free - John 8:32. A must read by my friend Bernadette."

DR. STELLA IMMANUEL

"Bernadette Smith has an important message for our time. Her focus on the importance of building unity amidst diversity as well as her daily application of timeless principles from scripture is a solid reminder of "whatever is true, whatever is noble, whatever is right, whatever is lovely, whatever is admirable-if anything is excellent or praiseworthy-think about such things. This book will be such a blessing to all that read it."

JOHN MOOLENAAR

(United States Congressman)

"If you want to hear about signs, wonders, and miracles, this is the book for you! Prophetic Utterances from the Holy Spirit & Words of Encouragement is full of delightful stories of my mom's walk with God. Growing up she was an excellent example of a woman, after God's own heart, and she continues to change people's lives by denying herself daily, taking up his cross, and serving him. I highly recommend you read this book, it's Phenomenal."

EDEN SMITH

(Self-learner)

"I have known Bernadette Smith and her family for many years. Her book, Prophetic Utterances from the Holy Spirit, is written by a true heroine. As pastors of their congregation, she, and her husband Philip, bravely stepped out during a time when our entire country was shut down to organize events that united people of all races and religions to stand for truth and to call this country back to our calling as "One nation under God indivisible with liberty and justice for all". They continue to work tirelessly to bring about positive change, an awakening, and a more clear understanding of our history and responsibility to the citizens of this great country. This book is a worthy read!"

JERRY R. WEINZIERL

(Pastor, Grace Christian Church)

"Rarely have we met a soul who lives as deeply in the word as Bernadette Smith. This book will inspire you to look deeper into what we see in truth. It is vital that we focus on what unites us and rise above what divides us and as Christian's in the body of Christ this book will help elevate you to rise up into His abundance, His power, and His authority.

Treasure the important messages within this book that will help you to learn how to trust in the Lord and lean not on our own understanding. May you also be blessed as you feel the impartation of the Holy Spirit lead you to His Glory as you read this book for 'such a time as this'!

God Bless,"

BO AND SOPHIA POLNY

(Gold2020forecast.com)

"My beautiful, sweet, and precious wife Bernadette has been telling me about these amazing encounters with God and Angels for many years. I am so honored to be her husband of nearly 33 years. I am so happy that she can share these amazing encounters with you. I hope you enjoy them as much as I have. Love and blessings, may God's richest and best always be yours."

PHILIP SMITH

Senior Pastor of Eternal Word Church

He Is Our Good Shepherd

I heard these words again out of my spirit:

The fire of the Holy Spirit is moving upon the face of the earth, burning everything that's not like God and bringing His plans to full completion.

Philippians 1:6 states "And I am convinced and sure of this very thing, that He who began a good work in YOU will continue until the day of Jesus Christ's return (right up to the time of His return).

He will be developing that good work and perfecting and bringing it to full completion in you.

The Lord WILL perfect that which concerns you. His mercy and loving-kindness endures forever. (Psalms 138:8).

When we cry out to our Heavenly Father, He performs on our behalf and rewards us. He will bring to pass His purposes for each and every one of us. He will perform on our behalf, and He will complete the purposes.

> *I will cry to the God Most High, who accomplishes all things on my behalf. (Psalms 57:2).*

Many people are concerned and worried about many things. They are worrying about what's happening in our country today and also about their own welfare.

I want to encourage you today, that the Lord will protect this country and He will protect and deliver you from worry, anxiety, concerns, and fears.

The Lord requires us ALL to seek, worship, praise, and thank Him. You may be asking, what am I seeking, worshipping, praising, and thanking Him for? It is because of who He is. He is the Almighty God, the Everlasting Father, and the Prince of Peace.

We worship and praise Him for what He has done and for what He is going to do.

He is our GOOD Shepherd

He is our Redeemer

He is our Deliverer

He is our Healer

He is our Peace

He is our Protector

He is our Shelter

He is our Provider

He is our Guide

He is our perfector,

and He is so MUCH MORE!!

I also want to encourage us all to stay in our own lane and stop trying to perfect ourselves. Jesus is our perfector. Our lane is to seek Him through prayer and the Holy Bible and then follow and obey what He instructs us to do. We will then begin to experience deliverance, revival, and TRUE peace.

Our precious and Heavenly Father will truly PERFECT everything that concerns us, and He will protect our country.

Love You ALL to Life!

DEFINITIONS:

COMPLETION = Fulfillment; accomplishment.

CONVINCED = Persuaded in mind; satisfied with evidence; convicted.

DEVELOPING = Unfolding; disclosing; unraveling.

PERFECTING = Finishing; completing; consummating.

PERFECT = Finished; complete; consummate; not defective; having all that is requisite to its nature and kind.

PERFORM = To do; to execute; to accomplish.

MERCY = Compassion or forgiveness shown toward someone whom it is within one's power to punish or harm.

LOVING-KINDNESS = Tenderness and consideration toward others.

ENDURES = To last; to continue in the same state without perishing; to remain; to abide.

REWARD = Recompense, or equivalent return for good, for kindness, for services, and the like. Rewards may consist of money, goods, or any return of kindness or happiness.

PROTECT = To cover or shield from danger or injury; to defend; to guard; to preserve in safety.

PROTECTOR = A defender; One that defends or shields from injury, evil, or oppression.

WELFARE = Exemption from misfortune, sickness, calamity, or evil; the enjoyment of health and the common blessings of life; prosperity; happiness.

DELIVERER = One who delivers; one who releases or rescues; a preserver.

WORRY = To give way to anxiety or unease; to allow one's mind to dwell on difficulty or troubles.

ANXIETY = Concern or solicitude respecting some event, future or uncertain, which disturbs the mind, and keeps it in a state of painful uneasiness.

FEAR = A painful emotion or passion excited by an expectation of evil, or the apprehension of impending danger.

SEEK = To make a search or inquiry; to endeavor to make the discovery.

SHEPHERD = God and Christ; They lead, protect and govern their people, and provide for their welfare.

REDEEMER = One who redeems or ransoms, The Savior of the world, JESUS CHRIST.

HEALER = He or that which cures or restores soundness.

PEACE = A state of quiet or tranquility; freedom from disturbance or agitation.

SHELTER = That which covers or defends from injury or annoyance.

PROVIDER = One who provides, furnishes, or supplies; one that procures what is wanted.

GUIDE = A person who leads or directs another in his way or course in life.

LANE = Your part; A narrow way or passage, or a private passage, as distinguished from a public road or highway.

FOLLOW = To come after another; To attend; to accompany.

OBEY = To hear God's Word and act accordingly; To comply with the commands, orders, or instructions of a superior.

INSTRUCT = To teach; to inform the mind; to educate; to impart knowledge to one who was destitute of it.

EXPERIENCE = The sum of practical wisdom taught by the events and observations of life; the personal and practical acquaintance with what is so taught.

REVIVAL = Recall, return, or recovery from a state of neglect, oblivion, obscurity, or depression; Recall, return, or recovery from a state of neglect, oblivion, obscurity, or depression

Our Foundation

The book of Proverbs tells us:

"The fear of the Lord is the beginning of knowledge" (Proverbs 1:7).

America's Founders certainly understood this truth, and from the beginning stressed the relationship between a SOUND EDUCATION based upon BIBLICAL ABSOLUTES and the future of the nation.

In 1776, the future President John Adams said, "Statesmen may plan and speculate for liberty, but it is religion and morality alone, which can establish the principles upon which freedom can securely stand." That mindset was widely held among the Founders who helped shape the POLITICAL, EDUCATIONAL, and LEGAL FOUNDATIONS of the new nation. Men such as Daniel Webster, Benjamin Franklin, Benjamin Rush, Samuel Adams, and George Washington echoed these same sentiments, believing that the strength of the REPUBLIC was dependent upon the MORALITY of her people, and that religion must undergird it. They saw the education of young minds being at the heart of it.

REPUBLIC was dependent upon the MORALITY of her people, and that religion must undergird it. They saw the education of young minds being at the heart of it.

Is it ironic today that our society is trying to destroy our children and young minds through immorality?

If history is erased and removed from our schools, colleges, and universities, then there will be no foundation to stand on. If there is no foundation to stand on, then we lose everything and become ruined and destroyed.

For no other foundation can anyone lay than that which is laid, which is Jesus Christ. (I Corinthians 3:11)

I want to encourage EVERYONE to educate yourselves, your family, your community, and your state regarding these truths.

Love you ALL to life!

DEFINITIONS:

KNOWLEDGE = A clear and certain perception of that which exists, or of truth and fact; the perception of the connection and agreement, or disagreement and repugnancy of our ideas.

ABSOLUTE = not qualified or diminished in any way; total; viewed or existing independently and not in relation to other things; not relative or comparative; "absolute moral standards"

SPECULATE = To meditate; to contemplate; to consider a subject by turning it in the mind and viewing it in its different aspects and relations; as to speculate on political events; to speculate on the probable results of a discovery; form a theory or conjecture about a subject without firm evidence.

RELIGION = Religion, in its most comprehensive sense, includes a belief in the being and perfections of God, in the revelation of his will to man, in man's obligation to obey his commands, in a state of reward and punishment, and in man's accountability to God, and also true godliness or piety of life, with the practice of all moral duties. It, therefore, comprehends theology, as a system of doctrines or principles, as well as practical piety; for the practice of moral duties without a belief in a divine lawgiver, and without reference to his will or commands, is not religion.

MORALITY = The doctrine or system of moral duties, or the duties of men in their social character; ethics; The quality of an action which renders it good; the conformity of an act to the divine law, or to the principles of rectitude. This conformity implies that the act must be performed by a free agent, and from a motive of obedience to the divine will. This is the strict theological and scriptural sense of morality. But we often apply the word to actions that accord with justice and human laws, without reference to the motives from which they proceed.

EDUCATE = To bring up, as a child; to instruct; to inform and enlighten the understanding; to instill into the mind principles of arts, science, morals, religion, and behavior. Educating children well is one of the most important duties of parents and guardians.

HISTORY = An account of facts, particularly of facts respecting nations or states; a narration of events in the order in which they happened, with their causes and effects. History differs from annals. Annals relate simply the facts and events of each year, in strict chronological order, without any observations of the annalist. History regards less strictly the arrangement of events under each year and admits the observations of the writer. This distinction however is not always regarded with strictness.

FOUNDATION = The basis or groundwork, of anything; that on which anything stands, and by which it is supported. A free government has its foundation in the choice and consent of the people to be governed. Christ is the foundation of the church. Behold, I lay in Zion for a foundation, a stone--a precious cornerstone. Isaiah 28. Other foundations can no man lay than that which is laid, which is Jesus Christ. 1 Corinthians 3.

SOCIETY = The union of a number of rational beings; or a number of persons united, either for a temporary or permanent purpose. Thus, the inhabitants of a state or of a city constitute a society, having common interests; hence it is called a community. In a more enlarged sense, the whole race or family of man is a society and called human society; the aggregate of people living together in a more or less ordered community.

TRUTH = God's Word (St. John 17:17); Conformity to fact or reality; exact accordance with that which is, or has been, or shall be. The truth of history constitutes its whole value. We rely on the truth of the scriptural prophecies.

STRESS = Give particular emphasis or importance to (a point, statement, or idea) made in speech or writing. "they stressed the need for reform Force; urgency; pressure; importance; that which bears with most weight; as the stress of a legal question. Consider how much stress is laid on the exercise of charity in the New Testament.

FEAR = Reverence; respect; due regard. Render to all their dues; fear to whom fear. (Romans 13).

RELATIONSHIP = The state of being related by kindred, affinity, or other alliance, a connection, association, or involvement.

SENTIMENT = A thought prompted by passion or feeling.

RUIN = To subvert; to destroy; as to ruin a state or government; To counteract; to defeat; as, to ruin a plan or project.

DESTROY = To demolish; to pull down; to separate the parts of an edifice, the union of which is necessary to constitute the thing; as to destroy a house or temple; to destroy a fortification; To ruin; to bring to naught; to annihilate; as to destroy a theory or scheme; to destroy a government; to destroy influence.

REPUBLIC = A commonwealth; a state in which the exercise of the sovereign power is lodged in representatives elected by the people. In modern usage, it differs from a democracy or democratic state, in which the people exercise the powers of sovereignty in person. Yet the democracies of Greece are often called.

IRONIC = Happening in the opposite way to what is expected, and typically causing wry amusement because of this; using or characterized by irony.

IMMORALITY = Any act or practice which contravenes the divine commands or the social duties. Injustice, dishonesty, fraud, slander, profaneness, gaming, intemperance, and lewdness are immoralities. All crimes are immoralities, but crime expresses more than immorality; the state or quality of being immoral; wickedness.

Stay Laser-Focused

I woke up this morning and heard these words out of my spirit:

"The Lord is a shield for me, my Glory and the lifter of my head"
(Psalms 3:3).

I then heard:

Stay laser focused and do not let distractions take you off the path of your destiny and your purpose in life.

We were ALL born for an amazing reason and for an amazing purpose.

When we were in the matrix of our mother's womb the Lord knew us. (Jeremiah 1:5)

We were all born to effect positive change in this world and as we look to Jesus, we will do just that.

It states in the book of Hebrews 12:2, "Looking away from all that will DISTRACT to Jesus, who is the leader and the source of our faith and also is the finisher (bringing it to maturity and perfection). He for the joy that was set before Him, endured the cross, despising and ignoring the shame, and is now seated at the right hand of the throne of God.

I want to encourage you all to not allow distractions of ANY KIND to take you off the course of your destiny and purpose in life or to distract you from finding your purpose in life.

Love you ALL to life!

DEFINITIONS:

SHIELD = To cover, as with a shield; to cover from danger; to defend; to protect; to secure from assault or injury.

GLORY = To exult with joy; to rejoice; high renown or honor won by notable achievements.

LIFTER = One that lifts or raises.

LASER FOCUS = The mental ability to give 100 percent of your attention to the task you've prioritized in the present moment. It helps you put aside all the delicious unrelated thoughts and sustain the energy required to reach your goals.

DISTRACT = Literally, to draw apart; to pull in different directions, and separate. Hence, to divide; to separate; and hence, to throw into confusion. Sometimes in a literal sense. Contradictory or mistaken orders.

DISTRACTION = Confusion from a multiplicity of objects crowding on the mind and calling the attention different ways; perturbation of mind; perplexity; as the family was in a state of distraction; a thing that prevents someone from giving full attention to something else.

PURPOSE = The reason for which something is done or created or for which something exists; That which a person sets before himself as an object to be reached or accomplished; the end or aim to which the view is directed in any plan, measure, or exertion. We believe the Supreme Being created intelligent beings for some benevolent and glorious purpose.

PATH = Course of life; the route or direction followed by a ship, aircraft, road, or river.

DESTINY = State or condition appointed or predetermined; ultimate fate; as men are solicitous to know their future.

MATRIX = The womb; the cavity in which the fetus of an animal is formed and nourished till its birth; The place where anything is formed or produced.

COURSE = A passing; a moving, or motion forward, in a direct or curving line; applicable to anybody or substance, solid or fluid; path.

WOMB = The uterus or matrix of a female; that part where the young of an animal is conceived and nourished till its birth. The organ in the lower body of a woman or female mammal where offspring are conceived.

KNEW = To know

KNOW = To perceive with certainty; to understand clearly; to have a clear and certain perception of truth, fact, or anything that actually exists. To know a thing precludes.

EFFECT = Cause (something) to happen; bring about; a change which is a result or consequence of an action or other cause.

MATURE = To advance towards ripeness; to become ripe or perfect.

MATURITY = Ripeness; a state of perfection.

SHAME = to be ashamed.

ASHAMED = Affected by shame; abashed or confused by guilt or a conviction of some criminal action or indecorous conduct, or by the exposure of some gross errors or misconduct, which the person is conscious must be wrong, and which tends to impair his honor or reputation.

The Joy of the Lord is Our Strength

Don't allow people or circumstances to steal your joy. If you lose your joy then you will lose your strength. If you lose your strength, then paralysis sets in. If paralysis sets in, then you become incapacitated, immobile, and ineffective in life.

I want to encourage you all to stand strong, unshakable with the truth, and with great courage.

Let the force of JOY penetrate your soul.

When you do this, you will live a life full of JOY, PEACE, CONTENTMENT, THANKFULNESS, EXCITEMENT, and COURAGE.

Love you ALL to life!

DEFINITIONS:

JOY = To gladden; to exhilarate; the passion or emotion excited by the acquisition or expectation of good; a feeling of great pleasure and happiness.

STRENGTH = Power or vigor of any kind; the power of resisting attacks; the power of the mind; that which supports; that which supplies strength; security; to withstand great force or pressure.

PARALYSIS = Inability to act or function in a person, organization, or place; the loss of the ability to move.

INCAPACITATED = To deprive of capacity or natural power of learning, knowing, understanding, or performing; to deprive strength or power.

IMMOBILE = Not moving; motionless; incapable of moving or being moved.

INEFFECTIVE = Not producing any effect, or the effect intended l; inefficient.

UNAFFECTED = Feeling or showing no effects or changes.

ENCOURAGE = To give courage; to give or increase the confidence of success; to inspire with courage, spirit, or strength of mind.

STRONG = Able to withstand great force or pressure.

UNSHAKABLE = That cannot be shaken; a belief or feeling or opinion is strongly felt and unable to be changed.

TRUTH = God's Word is Truth (St. John 17:17) Conformity to fact or reality.

COURAGE = The quality of mind which enables men to encounter danger and difficulties with firmness, or without fear or depression of spirits.

PENETRATE = To enter or pierce; To affect the mind; To make way.

SOUL = The spiritual, rational, and immortal substance in man, which distinguishes him from brutes; that part of man that enables him to think and reason, and which renders him a subject of moral government. The immortality of the soul is a fundamental article of the Christian system. The mind, Will, and emotion of a human.

PEACE = Freedom from agitation or disturbance by the passions, as from fear, terror, anger, anxiety, or the like; Quietness of mind; Tranquility; Calmness; Quiet of conscience; A state of quiet or tranquility.

CONTENTMENT = A resting or satisfaction of mind without disquiet; acquiescence; a state of happiness and satisfaction.

THANKFULNESS = The expression of gratitude; acknowledgment of favor; the feeling of being happy or grateful because of something.

EXCITEMENT = A feeling of great enthusiasm and eagerness; the state of being roused into action, or of having increased action; the act of excitement.

THERE IS A MENTAL WAR GOING ON

Satan is bringing evil & negative thoughts, ideas, and suggestions to people's minds. He (the devil) suggests to one's mind that people are speaking badly of them, that people do not like them.

He speaks and says: "You are going to die."

He speaks and says: "Give up, you will never win the battle that's raging against you."

He speaks and says: "You are not worthy of this or that."

He speaks and says: "There is no more hope for our state and our country."

He speaks and says: "We can't overcome this evil darkness."

Please know that the enemy is trying to get people to act out of their flesh towards people, towards situations, and towards circumstances that come to their minds or through others. THOUGHTS COME MANY TIMES IN PICTURES.

He is trying to bring a spirit of confusion, disunity, and hopelessness to everyone. He is trying to daily steal our peace and our joy; so that he can ultimately steal our strength.

He is trying to steal our strength to fight and stand for what is right, our strength to stand for our healing, and our strength to walk out our God-given destiny.

It is never good to act according to the flesh. We must act and respond according to the Word of God!

I am reminded of the scripture that says:

Casting down arguments and every high thing that exalts itself against the knowledge of God, bringing every thought into captivity to the obedience of Christ. (Corinthians 10:5)

I want to encourage everyone to pray and read the Holy Bible and get our Heavenly Father's perspective, truth, and answers to the war that's going on in the soulish realm, our body, our state, and our country.

When we act according to the truth of God's word, we will hit the target every time and we will live in PEACE, JOY, and VICTORY!!!

I say this often and want to say it again:

NEVER ALLOW TIME TO DETERMINE DEFEAT in our lives, in our circumstances, in our state, and in our country.

Love you ALL To life!

DEFINITIONS:

SUGGEST = Cause one to think that something exists or is the case; state or express indirectly.

SUGGESTIONS = Presentation of an idea to the mind; insinuation; secret notification or incitement.

IDEA = That considers ideas as images, phantasms, or forms in the mind.

EVIL = Profoundly immoral and wicked.

NEGATIVE = A proposition by which something is denied.

BATTLE = A fight or encounter between enemies; Fight or struggle tenaciously to achieve or resist.

TENACIOUSLY = With a firm hold of something; closely; in a determined or unwavering manner.

RAGING = Furry; violence; impetuosity; vehemently driven or agitated.

WORTHY = Deserving, such as merits; having worth or excellence.

HOPE = To desire with expectation of good; confidence in a future event; the highest degree of well-funded expectation of God.

ENEMY = A foe; an adversary; a person who is actively opposed or hostile to someone or something.

FLESH = A carnal state; a state of unrenewed nature; the corruptible body of man, or corrupt nature; the soft substance consisting of muscle and fat that is found between the skin and bones of an animal or human.

CONFUSION = A mixture of several things promiscuously; hence; disorder; irregularity; lack of understanding; the state of being bewildered or unclear in one's mind.

DISUNITY = A state of separation; disagreement and conflict within a group.

HOPELESSNESS = A feeling of despair; a state of being desperate or affording no hope.

PEACE = A state of quiet or tranquility, freedom from disturbance or agitation.

JOY = The passion or emotion excited by the acquisition or expectation of good; a glorious and triumphant state; to rejoice; to gladden; to exhilarate.

STRENGTH = Power or vigor of any kind; the power of resisting attacks; fastness; support.

ULTIMATELY = Finally; at last; at the end of last consequence.

DESTINY = State or condition appointed or predetermined, a necessity or fixed order of things established by a divine decree.

ARGUMENTS = An exchange of diverging or opposite views; typically, heated or angry one; A reason or set of reasons given with the aim of persuading others that an action or idea is right or wrong.

EXALTS = To raise high; to elevate; to elevate in power.

CAPTIVITY = The state of being a prisoner; being in the power of an enemy by force or the fate of war; a state of being under control.

PERSPECTIVE = A glass through which objects are viewed.

TRUTH = God's Word; Conformity to fact or reality.

SOUL = Mind, Will, emotion; The spiritual, rational, and immortal substance in man, which distinguishes him from brutes.

BRUTE = Senseless; unconscious.

TARGET = A shield or buckler of a small kind; used as a defensive weapon in war.

VICTORY = Conquest; the defeat of an enemy in battle, or of an antagonist in contest.

DETERMINE = To end; particularly; to end by the decision or conclusion.

DEFEAT = Overthrow; loss of battle; the check, rout, or destruction of an army by the victory of an enemy; win the victory over someone in battle or contest; overcome or beat.

TRUST

As I was meditating this morning, I heard these words:

All of those who devour you shall be devoured; those who plunder you shall become plundered and all who prey upon you I will make a prey! For I will restore health to you and heal you of your wounds.

I want to encourage everyone to put total trust in our Heavenly Father's ability to accomplish in and through us what He has called each and every one of us to do; and that we will ALL fulfill our purpose and destiny in this life. This is where true peace, joy, happiness, and contentment dwells!! Let us decree and declare that the Lord will heal wounds and bring health to each and EVERYONE; health to our HOUSEHOLD, health to our CITIES health to our STATE, and health to our COUNTRY!!

Love you ALL to life!

DEFINITIONS:

DEVOUR = To destroy; to consume.

PLUNDER = To rob as a thief; to steal; to take by open force.

PREY = The human subject of an attack or ridicule by another person.

RESTORE = To bring back or recover from lapse; to replace; to return as a person or thing to a former place.

WOUND = To inflict; to hurt; a wound given to credit or reputation.

ACCOMPLISH = To execute; to gain; to obtain or effect by successful exertions.

FULFILL = To accomplish what was intended; to perform; to complete.

PURPOSE = The reason for which something is done or created or for which something exists.

DESTINY = State or condition appointed or predetermined; A necessity or fixed order of things established by a divine decree.

PEACE = A state of quiet or tranquility; freedom from disturbance or agitation.

JOY = To gladden; to enjoy; to have or possess with pleasure.

HAPPINESS = The agreeable sensation which springs from the enjoyment of God.

CONTENTMENT = Content; a resting or satisfaction of mind without disquiet; gratification.

DWELL = To abide as a permanent resident, or to inhabit for a time, to live in a place.

DECREE = An official order issued by a legal authority, order by decree.

DECLARE = To make a declaration; to proclaim or avow some opinion or resolution in favor or in opposition; to make known explicitly some determination.

TRUTH

Doing the right thing may not always be easy, but it is always rewarding. Being a just person may not please everyone, but it is the right thing to do. If we are going to be effective and purposeful leaders of any kind, I want to encourage us all to seek the truth and do what is right.

Truth always prevails. It may not prevail when we think it should prevail, but it will.

Do not allow time to determine defeat. Time does not determine defeat!

Never compromise with the truth, but LIVE in the truth. How we deliver the truth is also VERY important.

I want to encourage those who are discouraged, weak, worried, in fear, and in despair to take courage and be at peace. The day of your vindication will come.

The day of vindication for our state and our country will come as well.

Keep pressing, standing, and fighting for what is right.

It is VITAL that we walk in UNITY as long as the unity is the truth. Unifying around our U.S. Constitution is imperative.

Our cities, our states, and our country needs us ALL.

Love you ALL to life!

DEFINITIONS:

EFFECTIVE = Having the power to cause or produce; Having the power of active operation; able; causing to be

PURPOSEFUL = Having or showing determination or resolve; determined; firm; steadfast; single-minded

TRUTH = Conformity to fact or reality; exact accordance with that which is, or has been, or shall be, Veracity; purity from falsehood; Honesty; Real fact of just principle; real state of things; Sincerity

PREVAIL = To overcome; to gain the victory or superiority; to gain the advantage, to have effect; power or influence; To succeed

DEFEAT = Overthrow; loss of battle; the check, rout, or destruction of an army by the victory of an enemy; To render null and void; To resist with success

DETERMINE = To end and fix; to settle ultimately; To settle or ascertain, as something uncertain; To resolve; to conclude; to come to a decision

COMPROMISE = Mutual agreement; adjustment; To adjust and settle a difference by mutual agreement

ENCOURAGE = To give courage to; to give or increase confidence of success; to inspire with courage, spirit, or strength of mind; to embolden; to animate; to incite; to inspire.

DISCOURAGE = To extinguish the courage of; to dishearten; to depress the spirits; to deject; to deprive of confidence; To attempt to repress or prevent; to dissuade from

WEAK = Yield, fail, give way, recede, or to be soft; Not having the force of authority or energy; easily broken; not healthy; not well supported by truth or reason

WORRIED = Harassed; fatigued

FEAR = A painful emotion or passion excited by an expectation of evil, or the apprehension of impending danger; Anxiety; To feel a painful apprehension of some impending evil; to consider or expect with emotions of alarm

DESPAIR = Hopelessness; a hopeless state; The destitution of hope or expectation

COURAGE = Bravery; intrepidity; that quality of mind which enables men to encounter danger and difficulties with firmness, or without fear or depression of spirits; valor; boldness; resolution.

PEACE = Freedom from agitation or disturbance by the passions, as from fear, terror, anger, anxiety, or the like; quietness of mind; tranquility; calmness; quiet of conscience

VINDICATION = The defense of anything, or a justification against denial or censure, or against objections or accusations; the proving of anything to be just; Defense by force or otherwise

VITAL = Contributing to life; necessary to life; Very necessary; highly important; essential

UNITY = The state of being one; oneness; Agreement.

IMPERATIVE = Commanding; expressive of command; containing positive command

LIVE = To continue constantly or habitually; to live a life of ease; to act habitually in conformity to.

THANKSGIVING

I want to honor our forefather Abraham Lincoln for issuing a proclamation on Oct. 3, 1863, declaring the last Thursday of November as a day of Thanksgiving. He saw the occasion as a peaceful interlude amid the Civil War.

I want to HONOR and THANK our Heavenly Father for sending His son, Jesus Christ, to the cross to pay for the sins of men.

Let us give thanks for this life-changing sacrifice that was paid for each and every one of us.

A thankful heart is a happy and joyful heart.

JOY brings us great strength. (Nehemiah 8:10)

We all need great strength and fortitude to stand strong and Bold during these times.

I am reminded of the verse that states:

Oh give thanks unto the Lord for He is good for His mercies endures forever. (Psalms 107:1)

We give thanks not necessarily because we feel like giving thanks, but because He said to give thanks. When we give thanks, we bring Our Heavenly into our circumstances. We don't give thanks FOR evil and bad things, but we give thanks IN them. When we give thanks because He is good, we bring Him into the mix, and when He gets into the mix everything changes for our good. GOODNESSES and MERCIES will overtake us and our circumstances.

Let us take time today and every day to give thanks unto the Lord! You will not be disappointed.

Love you ALL to life!

DEFINITIONS:

THANKSGIVING = The act of rendering thanks or expressing gratitude for favors or mercies.

THANKS = An expression of gratitude.

GOOD = That which contributes to diminish or remove pain; or to increase happiness or prosperity; Benefit; advantage; opposed to evil or misery.

MERCIES = Compassion or forgiveness shown toward someone whom it is within one's power to punish or harm; to treat an offender better than he deserves.

ENDURES = To last; to continue in the same state without perishing; to Remain; to abide.

FOREVER = For all future times; for always; continually; lasting or permanent.

STRENGTH = Power of resisting attacks; the power of the mind; intellectual force; spirit; the power of vigor of any kind; the quality of bodies by which they sustain the application of force without breaking or yielding.

FORTITUDE = That strength or firmness of mind or soul which enables a person to encounter danger with coolness and courage, or bear pain or adversity without murmuring depression, or despondency.

BOLDLY = In a bold manner; courageously; without timidity or fear; with confidence.

LET US GO OVER TO THE OTHER SIDE

Many are concerned about the future of our state and nation. Many are concerned about their lives. I am reminded of a story that the Lord told me many years ago.

I was greatly concerned about a few things, and I heard these words spoken to me by the Lord:

A deeper TRUST = a deeper REST.

He then reminded me of a Bible story.

The Lord said: Do you remember when I told the disciples to get into the boat and let's go over to the other side? (Mark 4:35-39)

I said: Yes Lord!

He then proceeded on and said: As we were going over on the other side, this great monstrous storm came upon the waters. The

47

water began to fill up inside the boat and the boat began to sink. The disciples cried out; we are perishing. They proceeded to go to the stern part of the boat to look for me. They found me fast asleep. They woke me up and said, "Master we are perishing"! I then got up and I rebuked the storm and the storm ceased.

Right after Jesus told me that story, He then asked me a very important question.

Jesus said to me: Bernadette, why was I able to rest in the midst of the storm?

Before I could answer Him back, He said to me: Because I TRUSTED My word; when I said that we are going over to the other side, we are going over.

He also said: When you learn to TRUST My words you will begin to rest in the midst of your storms.

I want to encourage us all, it does not matter what storms come our way in this life. It does not matter how the enemy is boasting himself so proudly saying "I got them now", "I got this state now", "I got this country now. "

NO HE DOES NOT!

Please know that we are going to make it safely to the other side in VICTORY!!

STAY THE COURSE, and do not give up!!!

He said to me: When you learn to trust My words instead of what you see and feel, and even smell, you will have a deeper rest.

Like the waves and water hitting the disciples to what has come against you in your life and what has come against our cities, our states and our country.

Jesus said that He will never leave us nor forsake us.
(Hebrews 13:5).

I want to encourage us all, that the light shines brighter in the darkness!

We are walking in uncharted times, but God is with us. He is an amazing guide. Let's allow Him to lead and guide us. We are coming safely on the other side.

The light in us will penetrate and destroy the dark and evil agenda of the enemy, as we use the authority that was given to us by our Heavenly Father.

Behold, I give you the authority to trample on serpents and scorpions, and over all the power of the enemy, and nothing shall by any means hurt you. (Luke 10:19)

Let's choose to believe and TRUST His word so that we can enter into that deeper REST.

Love you ALL to life!

DEFINITIONS:

TRUST = Confidence; a reliance or resting of the mind on the integrity, veracity, and Justice of another.

REST = Rest of body or mind; quiet; a state free from motion or disturbance; a state of reconciliation to God.

PERISHING = Suffer death, typically in a violent, sudden, or untimely way.

STERN = The hind part of a boat or ship.

REBUKED = Express sharp disapproval of someone because of their behavior.

PROCEED = Begin or continue a course of action; move forward.

MONSTROUS = Enormous; huge; extraordinary.

STORM = A violent wind; a tempest.

CEASE = To bring or come to an end.

UNCHARTED = (Of an area or land or sea) not mapped or surveyed; places not yet explored; unknown.

PENETRATE = To pass; to make way.

DESTROY = Put an end to the existence of something by damaging or attacking it.

AUTHORITY = The power or right to give orders, make decisions and enforce obedience.

THE RIGHT SIDE

As I was awakening this morning, I heard these words:

"Because the sentence against an evil work is not executed speedily, men's hearts are set to do evil". (Ecclesiastes 8:11)

Many people feel that because the day of execution and judgment has not come against their wickedness, their plots, their slanderous words, their cheating, their backbiting, and their sneakiness that they continue to walk in their evil doings.

I am reminded of the Bible verse that states: "The wicked plots against the JUST and gnashes at him with his teeth. The Lord laughs at him, for He sees that his day is coming. (Psalms 37: 12-13).

I believe that we are in the season that ALL wicked agendas, schemes, and plots by the enemy will be revealed and eradicated.

We need to make sure that we are not behind the evil or in support of the evil agendas in any way.

The Lord is long-suffering to all, so I am encouraging everyone to get on the RIGHT side (The Lord's side) and do what is right.

Love you ALL to life!

DEFINITIONS:

SCHEME = To make plans, especially in a devious way or with intent to do something illegal or wrong; A large-scale systematic plan or arrangement for attaining a particular object or putting a particular idea into effect.

JUDGMENT = A misfortune or calamity.

EXECUTED = To carry out or put into effect.

EVIL = Profoundly immoral and wicked.

WICKEDNESS = The quality of being evil or morally wrong; Departure from the rules of the divine law; Evil disposition or practices; Crime; Sin; Corrupt manners.

SLANDEROUS = False and Malicious (Of a spoken statement)

CHEATING = Act dishonestly or unfairly in order to gain an advantage.

BACKBITING = Malicious talk about someone who is not present.

SNEAKINESS = A disposition to be sly and stealthy and to do things surreptitiously.

PLOTS = A plan made in secret by a group of people to do something illegal or harmful.

REVEALED = Disclosed; discovered; made known; laid open; make (something) known to humans by divine or supernatural means.

ERADICATED = Destroyed completely; put an end to; plucked up by the roots; extirpated.

RIGHT = Conformity to the Will of God, or His law; the perfect standard of truth and justice.

JUST = Upright; honest; having principles of rectitude; conformed to the truth.

GNASHES = To grind the teeth; grind (one's teeth) together, typically as a sign of anger.

LONGSUFFERING = Having or showing patience in spite of troubles, especially those caused by other people.

VICTORY

As I was up praying, I heard these words:

NOTHING CAN WITHSTAND THE POWER OF GOD.

There are many demonic and evil forces that are lurking around the earth. They seem to be prevailing. I want you to know that none of those demonic and evil spirits can withstand the power of God.

We have been given the AUTHORITY and POWER to trample upon serpents and scorpions, and (physical and mental strength and ability) over ALL the power that the enemy (possess); and NOTHING shall in any way harm us. (Luke 10:19)

I want to encourage us all to be strengthened and encouraged. Stand strong, bold, and fearless, because when this war is all over, we will still be standing up in total VICTORY!!!

Love you All to life!

DEFINITIONS:

NOTHING = Not anything; not any being or existence; not any particular thing, deed, or event.

WITHSTAND = To oppose; to resist, either with physical or moral force; as to withstand the attack of troops; remain undamaged or unaffected by; resist.

POWER = Ability; strength; the faculty of moving or of producing a change in something.

GOD = The supreme being; Jehovah; the eternal and infinite spirit, the creator; and the Sovereign of the universe.

AUTHORITY = Delegated power; legal power or a right to command or to act.

TRAMPLE = To tread underfoot with contempt; to tread with force and rapidity; to tread on and crush.

HARM = Physical injury, especially that which is deliberately inflicted, Injury, hurt, damage, detriment.

PREVAILING = Gaining advantage; superiority or victory; having effect, persuading, succeeding.

LURKING = Remaining hidden; as to wait in ambush.

ENCOURAGED = To give courage; to give or increase the confidence of success; to embolden.

FEARLESS = Bold; courageous; intrepid; undaunted.

WE WIN

I have been meditating on Psalms 91:9-10. It states:

Because you have made the Lord your refuge, and the Most High your dwelling place, there shall NO evil befall you, nor any plague or calamity come near your tent.

I love how the GNB version states verse 10. It states:

He will keep you safe from ALL HIDDEN DANGERS and from ALL DEADLY DISEASES and so NO DISASTERS will strike you and NO VIOLENCE will come near your home.

I want to encourage us all to saturate ourselves, our families, our country, and our world with these verses.

You may have lost some battles (I have) but let's turn on the light of God's word and speak it and continue to speak it.

You too may have lost some battles, but I want you ALL to know that you will BIGLY win the WAR! When the dust settles, you will still be standing up in total VICTORY!!

Love you ALL To life!

DEFINITIONS:

DANGER = The possibility of suffering harm or danger.

DISASTER = A sudden event such as an accident or a natural catastrophe that causes great damage or loss of life.

DISEASE = A disorder or structure in a human body that impairs normal functioning & manifested by signs and symptoms (sickness) & Harmful developments.

VIOLENCE = Behavior involving physical force intended to hurt, Damage, or kill someone.

CALAMITY = An event causing great and often sudden damage or distress; a disaster.

SATURATE= Cause (something) to become thoroughly soaked with liquid so that no more can be absorbed.

DWELL = Live in or at a specified place

REFUGE = A condition of being safe or sheltered from pursuit, danger, or trouble.

HIDDEN = kept out of sight; concealed. "Hidden dangers"

VICTORY = an act of defeating an enemy or opponent in a battle, game, or other competition.

LOOK TO JESUS

There is a lot of noise and distractions going on in our world today!!

Many may be asking, how do I shut off all this noise and distractions that seem to be so prevalent in my mind and life?

I am reminded of the Bible verse in the book of Hebrews 12:2:
Looking unto Jesus, the author and finisher of our faith, who for the
joy that was set before Him endured the cross, despising the shame,
and has sat down at the right hand of the throne of God.

Looking away from ALL that will distract from Jesus, who is the Leader and the Source of our FAITH and is also the finisher of our faith.

The enemy is a master distractor and deceiver. He tries to keep us busy every moment of the day.

Why does he try to keep us busy? So that we cannot see the evil tricks and plans that he has done and is still trying to do against our lives and our country.

When we look away from distractions and look to Jesus (who is light and truth), He will help us to rightly navigate through the noise and distractions, which in return, will expose the enemy's evil tricks and plans.

The enemy wants to keep us enslaved and in darkness, but the truth and light will make us FREE.

I want to urge us ALL to look and keep looking to Jesus. He is such a masterful and loving guide.

Be encouraged and take comfort that we are on the winning team!!!

Love you ALL to life!

DEFINITIONS:

PREVALENT = Gaining advantage or superiority; predominant; powerful.

FAITH = Trust; belief; the assent of the mind to the truth of what is declared by another, resting on his authority and veracity without other evidence.

LEADER = One that leads or conducts, a guide.

SOURCE = First cause; original; a place, person, or thing from which something comes or can be obtained.

FINISHER = Bringing it to maturity and perfection.

DISTRACTOR = A person or thing that distracts.

TRUTH = God's Word (St. John 17:17); the quality or state of being true.

NOISE = To sound loud; Sound of any kind; frequent talk.

TRICKS = An artifice or stratagem for the purpose of deception; vicious practice.

PLAN = A detailed proposal for doing or achieving something.

NAVIGATE = To steer, direct or manage; plan and direct the route of a ship, aircraft or other forms of transportation, especially by using instruments or Maps.

FREE = Not enslaved; being in liberty; not being under necessity or restraint.

URGE = try earnestly or persistently to persuade (someone) to do something.

ENCOURAGE = To give courage to; to give or increase the confidence of success; to inspire with courage, spirit, or strength of mind.

COMFORT = To strengthen; to invigorate.

RIGHTLY = According to the divine Will or moral rectitude; honestly, correctly; properly.

MASTERFUL = Performed or performing very skillfully.

LOVING = Feeling or showing love or great care.

PRAY THE WORD OF GOD

I heard in my spirit:

Babylon the Great is falling!!

If you're not on the Lord's side, get on His side and stay put!

For God so loved the world that He gave His only begotten Son, that whoever believes in Him should not perish but have everlasting life. (St. John 3:16)

If you're on His side, you do not have to tremble and live in fear at what's going on in our world today or what's coming in the days ahead.

We are protected and secured in Jesus! We have our peace through Him. Let's keep our eyes fixed on Him. Let's pray and listen to Him and then obey what He tells us to do. Let's follow His method of operation.

Psalms 91:1-2 states: He that dwells in the secret place of the most high, shall abide under the shadow of the Almighty. I will SAY of the Lord, He is my refuge and my fortress, my God; on Him, I lean and rely, and in Him I confidently trust.

You may be asking, what is the secret place? The secret place is the place of prayer. You may also be asking, what do I pray?

We must pray the Word of God. Now this is the confidence that we have in Him, that if we ask anything according to His will, He hears us. (I. John 5:14)

> *Our Heavenly Father's divine power has given to us ALL things*
> *(through His word), that pertain to life and godliness. (2 Peter 1:3)*

When we are hidden under the shadow of the Almighty, the darkness cannot find us.

Please be encouraged and know that the light that's upon us will blind the enemy from destroying us.

Love you ALL to life!

DEFINITIONS:

SECRET PLACE = The place of prayer; to live with a constant awareness of God's presence in our life. When we enter that place of prayer, we enter into a knowledge of God which will repair or restore us.

ABIDE = To wait for; to be prepared; remain stable; fixed; to rest or dwell.

SHADOW = Shelter; protection; favor

REFUGE = Shelter or protection from danger or distress.

FORTRESS = A fortified place; a place of defense; safety; security; to guard.

LEAN = To bend or incline; so as to rest on something.

RELY = To rest on something, as the mind when satisfied of the veracity, integrity, or ability of persons; to trust in; to depend on.

CONFIDENTLY = With firm trust; with strong assurance; without doubt or wavering of opinion.

TRUST = Confidence; a reliance or resting of the mind on the integrity, veracity, justice;

the sound principle of another person.

HIDDEN = Kept out of sight; concealed.

BLIND = Destitute of the sense of seeing, either by natural defect or by deprivation, not having sight.

THE LORD IS WITH US

I was reminiscing over the words that I heard from my spirit:

The Lord is with us!

- On July 5, 2022, I heard: The Lord is with us.

- On July 11, 2022, I heard: The Lord is with us.

- On July 13, 2022, I heard: The Lord is with us.

- On July 14, 2022, I heard: The Lord is with us.

- On July 16, 2022, I heard: The Lord is on my side, I will not fear because God is with us.

- On July 23, 2022, I heard: God is with us.

- On July 26, 2022, I heard: The Lord is with us.

- On July 29, 2022, I heard: Who's on the Lord's side?

The Lord wants us ALL to know that HE is with us.

Throughout the word, the Lord assures us that HE is with us and that He will never leave us nor forsake us. He will not forsake our city, our state and our country.

Many are weighed down with oppression, fear & anxiety, and concern about many things.

I want us all to know that our help comes from the Lord, the maker of heaven and earth.

There is no need for us to fear or worry.

THE LORD IS WITH US. He will not leave or forsake us.

Let's make sure that we stay on His side.

The Lord said that He is near to ALL who call on Him. To all who call upon Him in truth (Ps. 145:18)

It doesn't matter how dark things are in your life or in our state and country, let's cry out to God and He promised that He will deliver us. Even when we cannot feel God, know that He is with us. You may ask, why is God with us? Because He said so.

I Peter 5:7 states: Casting the WHOLE of your care (all of your anxieties, all of your concerns, all of your worries) once and for all on Him for He cares for you affectionately and cares about you watchfully.

Matthew 1:23 states: Behold the virgin shall conceive and best a son, and they shall call His name Immanuel (which means, God with us).

Deuteronomy 4:31 states: For the Lord God is a merciful God; He will not abandon or destroy you....

Philippians 4:6-7 states: Do not be anxious for anything, but in everything by prayer and petition, make your request known unto God.

Why? Because God is with us!!!

God does not abandon us to navigate life on our own, but He, the Holy Spirit guides, comforts, and intercedes for us. We must work and follow His lead.

Let us ALL allow the Lord to govern our lives so that we can live in total peace, ok?

Please take comfort and courage that Our Heavenly Father is WITH US!!

Love you ALL to life!

DEFINITIONS:

REMINISCING = Indulge in enjoyable recollections of past events.

FORSAKE = Abandon someone or something; to forsake entirety; to renounce; to give up.

IMMANUEL = God with us.

AFFECTIONATELY = Passion, gentle; a gentle feeling of fondness or living tenderness.

WATCHFUL = Watching or observing someone or something closely; alert; vigilant.

ABANDON = Cease to support or look after; give up completely.

DESTROY = Put an end to the existence of something by damaging or attacking it; ruin; defeat.

PEACE = Freedom from disturbance and agitation; A state of quiet or tranquility; freedom from internal commotion.

INDEPENDENCE DAY

Why do we celebrate the 4th of July and what does it mean? This day is very significant in American history. It is the day that the United States officially became its own nation. The Declaration of Independence was adopted on July 4th, 1776, and at that time, America was born.

I want to share with you a little history of how it all began!

Before America was its own country, it comprised 13 colonies established by Great Britain. The first colony was settled in Jamestown and Virginia in 1607. European countries, especially Great Britain, continued to colonize America throughout the 17th century and a good portion of the 18th century. By 1775, an estimated 2.5 million settlers lived in the 13 colonies. New Hampshire, Massachusetts, Connecticut, Rhode Island, Delaware, New York, New Jersey, Pennsylvania, Maryland, Virginia, North Carolina, and Georgia.

Tensions started brewing when Great Britain began passing legislation that gave it more control within the colonies, especially when it came to taxing the colonists. The Crown was in debt after the French and Indian War, so it started taxing the American colonies to increase revenue. The passage of legislation like the Stamp Act in March 1765, the Townshend Act in June and July of 1767, and the Tea Act of 1773 forced colonists to pay more money to Great Britain even though the colonies didn't have a say in the Crown's Policies. This became known as taxation without representation and quickly became a heated pillar in the foundation of the American Revolution. This led the colonists to seek independence.

This day is the day that we celebrate our FREEDOMS and our GREAT COUNTRY. Let us stand and continue to stand against the tyranny that is trying to be placed upon ALL of us. We have fought too hard with wisdom from God and we have come too far, to allow our FREEDOMS to be taken away from us. We MUST not allow our Constitutional rights to be destroyed and taken away from us.

I want to thank ALL the soldiers who fought and gave their lives for the freedom of our country!!

I want to encourage us all to keep in our hearts and minds that true FREEDOM is knowing, accepting, and walking out what Jesus Christ did at the cross. All other FREEDOMS DERIVES from this FREEDOM. Our Lord and Savior shed His precious blood for us ALL. He paid the price so that we can all be FREE from any and everything that we need saving and freedom from.

Love you ALL To life!

DEFINITIONS:

FREEDOM = A state of exemption from the power or control of another; liberty; exemption from slavery; servitude or confinement.

COLONY = A company or body of people transplanted from their mother country to a remote province or country to cultivate and inhabit it.

COLONIST = An inhabitant of a colony.

TYRANNY = Cruel and oppressive government or rule; a nation under a cruel and oppressive government.

DERIVES = Obtain something from (a specific source); base a concept on a logical extension or modification of another concept.

REVENUE = Income; a state's annual income from which public expenses are met.

LEGISLATION = Laws considered; collectively

FOUNDATION = An underlying basis or principle.

REVOLUTION = A forcible overthrow of a government or social order; in favor of a new system.

FREE = Being in liberty; not being under necessity or restraint; not enslaved

SAVING = preserving from evil or destruction; hindering from waste or loss.

GOD IS AT WORK MENDING US

As I was waking up, I heard these words from my spirit:

God is picking up ALL the BROKEN pieces in us and in our lives and He is MENDING them.

I lay there a while and then began to meditate on those words. I want you all to pay close attention to what the word "mending" means. It means to repair; to supply a part broken or defective; to correct; to set right; to alter for better; to help; to advance; to improve; to improve morally.

GOD IS AT WORK MENDING US!!!

Our Heavenly Father has great and mighty plans for each and every one of us, for our state and for our country. Be encouraged and do not lose heart. Let us ALL fix our eyes on our savior Jesus Christ. Let's listen to His strategies and then put the strategies to practice. Do not fear and be anxious. It is all going to be ok!!!

I am reminded of the verse that says: *For I know the plans that I have for you. For I know the thoughts that I think towards you, says the Lord, thoughts of peace and not of evil, to give you a future and a hope. Then you will call upon Me and go and pray to Me, and I will listen to you. (Jeremiah 29:11-12).*

Again, be encouraged, and do not lose heart! Obey and everything is going to be ok!!

Love you ALL to life!

DEFINITIONS:

BROKEN = Having been fractured or damaged and no longer in one piece or in working order; having given up all hope:"; despairing; rent asunder.

STRATEGIES = A plan of action or policy designed to achieve a major overall aim; a plan for military operations and movements during war and battles.

FEAR = a painful emotion or passion excited by an expectation of evil.

ANXIOUS = Greatly concerned; being in painful suspense.

PEACE = A state of quiet or tranquility; freedom from disturbance or agitation.

PLANS = A detailed proposal for doing or achieving something.

FUTURE = That is to be or come after; that will exist at any time after the present.

HOPE = A feeling of expectation and desire for a certain thing to happen.

EVIL = Profoundly immoral and wicked.

OUR PRAYERS HAVE BEEN ANSWERED

The Supreme Court ruled that Roe vs. Wade be overturned. The author of death has been defeated and the author of LIFE has won the victory!!

In our great state of Michigan, our legislatures passed the law, which was then signed by the Governor, stating that it's a crime to assist with an abortion.

We must hold our legislatures and our Governor accountable for keeping this law.

Let us not allow ourselves and our government to overturn our Michigan law regarding abortion. We will not be ruled by the wicked and barbaric practice of abortion.

We must CONTINUE to rise up and be the state that values and protect LIFE, just like our creator values LIFE. Jesus said that the thief comes only to steal, kill and destroy, but that He came that we ALL may have LIFE and that we may ALL have it more abundantly (St. John 10:10).

Let us also pray and intercede in prayer that ALL states would honor and protect the LIFE of the unborn.

Love you ALL to life!

DEFINITIONS:

WICKED = Evil in principle or practice; deviating from the divine law.

BARBARIC = Savagely cruel; exceedingly brutal

DEFEATED = Having been beaten in battle; demoralized and overcome by adversity.

LIFE = The existence of an individual human being or animal.

VALUE = A person's principles or standards of behavior, The regard that something is held to deserve.

PROTECT = To keep safe from harm or Injury; to preserve.

RULE = Control of or dominion over an area of people.

CONTINUE = To persist in an activity or process, to preserve; not to cease to do or use.

INTERCEDE = Intervene on behalf of another.

PRAY = To ask with earnestness or zeal.

JUNETEENTH

Juneteenth is a federal holiday in the United States commemorating the emancipation of enslaved African Americans. Juneteenth marks the anniversary of the announcement of General Order No. 3 by Union Army General Gordon Granger on June 19, 1865, proclaiming freedom for enslaved people in Texas.

Many soldiers placed their lives on the line during the civil war to bring an end to slavery, along with the abolitionists. On January 1, 1863, President Lincoln formally issued the Emancipation Proclamation, calling on the Union army to LIBERATE ALL enslaved people in states still in rebellion as "an act of Justice, warranted by the constitution, upon military necessity". Three million enslaved people were declared to be free. In 1865 the 13th Amendment was formally adopted in the United States Constitution. The ending of slavery ENABLED many African Americans to move into their purpose and destiny in life. Because of this FREEDOM, many innovations were brought into our world and lives. I want to honor and celebrate them ALL. I also want to point out a few of them and their accomplishments.

---

[4] Wikipedia: Juneteenth

George Washington Carver was born on January 1, 1864, in Diamond, MO. He was an AMERICAN agricultural scientist and inventor who promoted alternative crops to cotton and methods to prevent soil depletion. He was one of the most prominent scientists of the early 20th century. He was also an educator and was famous for many inventions, including over 300 uses for the peanut.

Sarah Goode was born in 1855 in Toledo, Ohio. In 1888 Sarah applied for and was granted a patent in Chicago, Illinois. She conceptualized what she called the cabinet bed. This bed was designed to fold out into a writing desk to increase the demands of urban living in small spaces. She invented the cabinet bed "so as to occupy less space and made it generally to resemble some article of furniture when folded". She reimagined the domestic space to make city living more efficient.

Some other African American Inventors were:

- Garrett Augustus Morgan Sr., who invented the three-position traffic signal.

- Sarah Boone, Invented the ironing board

- Thomas L. Jennings, the patent for the method of dry cleaning.

- Ellen Eqlin, Invented the clothes wringer for washing machines.

- Miriam E. Benjamin, Invented a gong and signal chair.

- Henry Blair, Invented the seed planter and cotton planter

---

[5] Wikipedia: George Washington Carver
[6] Wikipedia: Sarah E. Goode

I want to point out how we ALL NEED each other, whether we are red, yellow, black, white, or brown skin. Let us help each other see this TRUTH.

Without the help of the Lord working through President Abraham Lincoln, the soldiers, and the abolitionists during the civil war, we would probably still be enslaved and in bondage; and without these GREAT inventors inventing these amazing and beneficial inventions, we would not be where we are today. You see, we are all helpers one to another and we need each other.

We have all come too far to lose what we have fought for. THAT IS OUR FREEDOM.

- Freedom of religion
- Freedom of speech
- Freedom to assemble
- Freedom of the press
- Freedom to pursue the American Dream
- Freedom to live in a free market system
- Freedom to bear arms (etc.)

We ALL bleed red.

Let us take time to focus on what has united us, and RISE above what is trying to divide and separate us.

Love you ALL to life!

DEFINITIONS:

CONCEPTUALIZED = To form a concept

INSURMOUNTABLE = To great to be overcome

ENABLED = To supply with the means, knowledge, or opportunity (to do something); make able; to make feasible or possible.

INNOVATION = This is the Creation, development, and implementation of a new product, process, or service, with the aim of improving efficiency, effectiveness, or competitive advantage.

ABOLITIONIST = A person who sought to abolish slavery during the 19th century. Most early abolitionists were white, religious Americans, but some of the most prominent leaders of the movement were black men and women who have escaped bondage

LIBERATE = To set free from a situation, especially slavery and imprisonment.

INNOVATION = To make changes in something established especially by introducing new methods, ideas, or products.

FREEDOM = A state of exemption from the power or control of another; Liberty exemption from slavery.

GOD IS THE REFUGE OF HIS PEOPLE AND THE CONQUEROR OF THE NATIONS

God is our refuge and strength. A very PRESENT help in trouble. Therefore, we will not fear, even though the earth be removed, and though the mountains be carried into the midst of the sea; though its waters roar and be troubled, though the mountains shake with its swelling. There is a river whose streams shall make glad the city of God, the holy place of the Tabernacle of the MOST HIGH.

God is in the midst of her, she shall not be moved; God shall help her, just at the break of dawn. The nations raged, the kingdoms were moved; He uttered His voice, and the earth melted.

THE LORD OF HOSTS IS WITH US; The God of Jacob is our refuge.

BE STILL and know that I am God; I will be exalted on the earth!!
THE LORD OF HOST IS WITH US; The God Jacob is our refuge.
(Psalms 46:1-7, 10-11)

I want us ALL to be encouraged and know that our Heavenly Father is not sitting around twisting his fingers. He is with us. He has given us everything to subdue our enemies. He paid the price for us through His blood at Calvary and He gave us The AUTHORITY and the POWER in His name. His name is the name above ALL names. I want to encourage us all to exercise the authority that He has given us; understanding that *we are NOT wrestling against flesh and blood, but against the master spirits who are the world rulers of this present darkness, against the spiritual forces of wickedness in the heavenly (supernatural) sphere. (Ephesians 6:12)*

Love you ALL to life!

DEFINITIONS:

REFUGE = To shelter and protect from danger and distress.

STRENGTH = Power of resisting attacks; that which supplies strength; security; the power of vigor of any kind.

FEAR = A painful emotion or passion excited by an expectation of evil, or the apprehension of impending danger; to be afraid.

PRESENT = Being in a certain place; as opposed to absent; being before the face or near; ready at hand; quick in an emergency.

HELP = To aid; to assist; to lend strength or means towards effecting a purpose.

TROUBLE = To agitate; to disturb; to put into confused motion; to afflict; to grieve; to distress: anxious.

ROAR = To cry with a full, loud, continuous sound; to make a loud noise.

BE STILL = Stop striving, stop fighting; relax; stop trying to defend yourself.

EXALTED = Raised to a lofty height, elevated, honored with office or rank; extolled.

MOST HIGH = God

CONQUEROR = One who conquers; one who gains a victory; one who subdues and brings into subjection or possession by force or by influence.

CONQUER = To overcome; to gain victory.

AUTHORITY = Legal power, or the right to command or to act; delegated power.

POWER = The capacity or ability to direct or influence the behavior of others or the course of events; the ability to do something or act in a particular way.

SUBDUE = To conquer by force or exertion of superior power and bring into permanent subjection.

WE ARE AT A RED SEA MOMENT

As I was meditating on the word this morning, I heard these words:

We are at a Red Sea moment!

Just like the Lord departed the Red Sea for the children of Israel, He will depart it for YOU, and our NATION!! (Exodus 14:21-31)

Many people are concerned and worried about what's happening in our state and our country today.

I want to share with you a word that the Lord continues to place on my heart for you all.

He said to be STRONG, BOLD, and COURAGEOUS for the Lord your God is with YOU. He is with YOU wherever YOU go.

Joshua 1:9 states: Have not I commanded you? Be STRONG, VIGOROUS and very COURAGEOUS. Be NOT afraid, neither be dismayed, for your God is with you wherever you go.

I want to also encourage you all to keep before you the light and to speak the light, which is God's word.

Remember LIGHT always dispels the DARKNESS.

It will dispel ALL of the enemy's schemes, plots, trickery, and plans against you, your family, and this nation.

God is light and in Him is NO darkness at all. (I John 1:5)

So let us all join together and rise up in FAITH and do not shrink in fear. Do not GO INTO HIDING! We will reach our promised land.

Love you ALL to life!

DEFINITIONS:

STRONG = Having the ability to bear or endure; well-fortified, able to sustain attacks; not easily subdued or taken.

VIGOROUS = Full of physical strength or active force; powerful; made by strength, either of body or mind.

COURAGEOUS = Brave; Bold, daring; hardy to encounter difficulties and dangers.

BOLD= Daring; courageous; fearless; brave; requiring courage in the execution; executed with spirit or boldness; confident.

Remember the Lord said for us not to be afraid or dismayed.

AFRAID = Impressed with fear or apprehension, fearful.

DISMAYED = Disheartened; deprived of courage.

TRICKERY = The practice of deception.

PROMISE LAND = A place or situation in which someone expects to find great happiness.

MOMENT = The most minute & indivisible part of the time; force; impulsive power; important in influence or effect.

MOTHER'S DAY

Mothers seem to be built with a supernatural Inner Strength! That Strength is given to us by our Heavenly Father.

Mothers are, for the most part, nurturers. As a mother of 8 children, I have seen the importance of being a nurturer. We provide meals, support, care, comfort, encouragement, and training to our children. We help mold and develop their character. We are all faced and have been faced with attacks, storms, and trials in our lives, but how we handle these attacks is key.

Psalms 34:19 states: *Many are the affliction of the righteous, but the Lord delivers them out of them all.*

I have experienced first-hand how it feels to be falsely accused of an attempt to assassinate one's character and at the same time have a young child fighting for her life in the ICU. The pressure can be extremely intense and overwhelming but staying close and true to the Word of God gave me that supernatural strength through it all. That strength gave me the ability to continue to raise my children in truth and honor. I used those attacks, storms, and trials as a teachable time for my children.

We must stay true to what is right and what is right is the word of God. (John 17:17)

Mothers you may be going through a storm or trials today. I want you to know that you are going to come out on the other side with comfort and victory. Be encouraged and stand strong in the liberty that was given to you through Christ Jesus.

Stand **BOLD** and UNAFRAID against the darkness.

I also want to encourage mothers and everyone not to allow their past attacks, trials, or storms to determine their future.

Let your life be governed by the Word of God. It will truly DIRECT and make straight and plain your path.

> *Trust in the Lord with all your heart and lean not on your own understanding; In all your ways acknowledge Him, and He shall direct your paths. (Proverbs 3:5-6)*

YOUR FUTURE IS VERY BRIGHT!!!

Love you ALL to life!

DEFINITIONS:

BOLD = Confident and courageous

UNAFRAID = Feeling no fear or anxiety.

BRIGHT = Promising good or success.

MOLD = To influence the formation or development of.

BOLD = Confident and courageous

UNAFRAID = Feeling no fear or anxiety.

BRIGHT = Promising good or success.

MOLD = To influence the formation or development of.

DEVELOP = Grow or cause to grow and become more mature, advanced, or elaborate.

CHARACTER = The mental and moral qualities distinctive to an individual.

GOVERN = Conduct the policy, actions, and affairs of a state, organization, or people.

DIRECT = Extending or moving one place to another in the shortest way.

PATH = Course of life.

INNER STRENGTH = Mental resistance to doubt or discouragement; resoluteness if will; integrity of character.

SUPERNATURAL = Of a manifestation attributed to some force beyond scientific understanding or laws of nature.

NURTURES = To feed; to nourish; to educate, to bring it to train up.

SUPPORT = Hold up; to give assistance to.

COMFORT = A state of physical ease and freedom from pain or constraints. The easing of alleviation of a person's feelings of grief or distress.

ENCOURAGEMENT = The action of giving someone support, confidence, or hope.

TRAINING = The action of teaching a person or animal a particular skill or type of behavior.

ATTACK = An aggressive and violent action against a person or place.

TRIAL = Experience; Suffering that puts strength, patience, or faith to the test.

STORMS = Affliction, calamity; distress; adversity.

AFFLICTIONS = A state of pain, distress, or grief.

DELIVER = To free, to release, to rescue.

ACCUSED = To charge with; or declare to have committed a crime; To charge with a fault; to blame.

ASSASSINATE = A murder (an important person) in a surprise attack for political or religious reasons.

INTENSE = Very severe or keen

OVERWHELMING = Very great in amount.

LIFE IS PRECIOUS

Life is such a precious gift given to ALL, from our Heavenly Father and we must PROTECT it.

> *Children are a HERITAGE from the Lord; the fruit of the WOMB is a reward! (Psalms 127:3)*

Join me in praying and decreeing that Roe V. Wade be overturned in this generation. For too long have we watched babies being murdered. The safest place for babies should be in the womb of their mother. An estimated 62 million babies have been aborted since the passing of Roe V. Wade in 1973.

Pray that the Supreme Court judges hold to their right decision and conviction in overturning Roe V. Wade. It was probably leaked in hopes that one of the Supreme Court Judges will change their mind. I believe that what the enemy meant for evil, will turn around for good.

St. John 10:10 states: The thief (the enemy of darkness) comes to steal, kill and destroy, but Jesus (the author of light and who is light) said that He came that we ALL may have LIFE and have it more abundantly (to the fullness).

Let's rally and continue to rally around this TRUTH.

The author of death is defeated, and the author of life has won the victory!!!!

WE WERE ALL BORN FOR THIS TIME!!

Love you ALL to life!

DEFINITIONS:

LIFE = The existence of an individual, human being, or animal.

PROTECT = To keep safe from harm or injury; to preserve.

WOMB = The uterus or matrix of a female; that part where the young of an animal is conceived and nourished till its birth.

GIFT = A thing given willingly to someone without payment.

HERITAGE = Inheritance; An estate that passes from an ancestor to an heir by descent or course of law; that which is inherited.

DECREE = Judicial decision or determination of a litigated case; a decision of a court of law.

LEAKED = Of secret made public; An intentional disclosure of something secret or private.

STEAL = To take without permission or legal right and without intending to return it.

KILL = Cause of death of a person, animal, or other living thing.

DESTROY = To put an end to the existence of something by damaging or attacking it.

LIGHT = The natural agent that stimulates sight and makes things visible.

DARKNESS = The absence of light; wickedness or evil.

ABUNDANTLY = In large quantities; plentifully.

RALLY = To come together again in order to continue fighting after a defeat or dispersion.

TRUTH = The quality or state of being the truth; God's Word is truth (St. John 17:17).

DEFEATED = Having been beaten in a battle or contest; demoralized and overcome by adversity.

VICTORY = An act of defeating an enemy or opponent in battle.

ALL AUTHORITY

May your day be filled with the peace, love, gratitude, and the joy of our Lord and Savior Jesus Christ!!!

Jesus died so that we can live!

What was the purpose and the power of Jesus' death and resurrection? The w1 purpose of the cross was to bring us ALL back into fellowship (Right standing) with God. We were ALL dead in sin and without hope (Ephesians 2:1). Adam brought us into sin, but Jesus paid the price to bring us back into right standing with Him.

> *Romans 5:17, states: For if by one man's (Adam) offense death reigned by one, much more they which receive abundance of grace and of the gift of righteousness shall reign in life by one Jesus Christ.*

After Jesus rose from the dead, He met His Disciples in Galilee and spoke to them and said "ALL AUTHORITY has been given to me in Heaven and on Earth". Go therefore and make disciples of all nations, baptizing them in the name of the Father, and of the Son, and of the Holy Spirit. Teaching them to observe ALL things that I have commanded you; And lo, I am with you ALWAYS, even to the end of the age (Matthew 28:17-20).

Jesus gave us back the authority that we once lost. Let us arise NOW and BOLDLY take the authority that He has given to us. Let us exercise this power through prayer over all of the wicked schemes, trickery, plots, and demonic forces that are coming against our states, our country, and our world today. If we do not take our authority through prayer over the darkness, the darkness will take authority over us. Let us be willing and ready to lead those who are not born of God, to Him.

Love you ALL to life!

DEFINITIONS:

RESURRECT = To bring a person back to life.

RESURRECTION = A rising again.

RIGHT STANDING = Being regarded as having done righteously and justly by God.

HOPE = A desire for some good, accompanied by a slight expectation.

GRACE = The unmerited gift of the divine favor of God.

RIGHTEOUSNESS = The quality of being morally right or justifiable.

REIGN = Rule as king or queen; to possess or exercise sovereign power.

AUTHORITY = Legal power, or a right to command or to act.

SCHEME = Make plans, especially in a devious way or with the intent to do something illegal or wrong.

TRICKERY = The practice of deception.

PLOTS = Secretly make plans to carry out an illegal or harmful action.

REIGN = Rule as king or queen; to possess or exercise sovereign power.

RISEN = Move from a lower position to a higher one. Come up or go up.

OBSERVE = Notice or perceive (something) and register it as being significant.

COMMAND = Give an authoritative order; A strategic position from a superior height.

NATION = A large body of people United by common descent, history, culture, or language inhabiting a particular country or territory.

BOLDLY = confidently and courageously.

DO NOT FEAR

In 1775, the Lutheran pastor John Peter Gabriel Muhlenberg preached a sermon on Ecclesiastes 3:1, "To everything, there is a season, a time for every purpose under heaven."

Concluding the message, he declared, "In the language of the Holy Writ, there is a time for all things. There is a time to PREACH and a time to FIGHT. NOW is the time to fight." He then threw off his clerical robes to reveal the uniform of a Revolutionary Army officer. That afternoon, at the head of 300 men, he matched off to join General Washington's troops and became Colonel of the 8th Virginia Regiment.

Ministers turned the colonial resistance into a righteous cause and served at every level of the conflict, from military chaplains to members of state legislatures to taking up arms and leading troops into battle. And, ultimately, after two main British armies were captured by the Continental Army at Saratoga in 1777 and Yorktown in 1781, the other words of Patrick Henry to his fellow Virginians proved true: "Three million people, armed with the holy cause of liberty, and in such a country as that which we possess, are invincible by any force which our enemy can send against us."

It is time for pastors, spiritual leaders, all leaders, and all people to ARISE and stand against all of the TYRANNY that is being afflicted in our state, our country, and our world today.

We must NOT fear, but BOLDLY rise up in FAITH like never before.

Always remember this, when we fear we are allowing tyranny to consume us. When we do not fear, it is a sure sign of our victory and Satan's defeat.

Philippians 1:28 states: And do not (for a moment) be frightened or intimidated in anything by your opponents and adversaries, for such (constancy and fearlessness) will be a clear sign (proof and seal) to them of their impending destruction, but a (sure token and evidence) of your deliverance and salvation, and that from God.

Love you ALL to life!

DEFINITIONS:

ARISE = To begin to act; to stand up; to move to a higher place.

STAND = To stop; to succeed; to maintain one's ground; Supported by the roots

TYRANNY = Arbitrary or despotic exercise of power; cruel government or discipline; absolute monarchy cruelly administered.

FEAR = A painful emotion or passion excited by an expectation of evil, or the apprehension of impending danger; anxiety, terrified, affright torment.

FAITH = Complete trust or confidence in someone or something; a strong belief in God.

AFFLICTED = Affected with continued or often repeated pain, either of body or mind; suffering grief or distress of any kind.

BOLDLY = In a bold manner; courageously; without timidity or fear; with confidence.

CONSUME = To waste away slowly; to be exhausted.

FRIGHTENED = Afraid or anxious.

INTIMIDATED = Made fearful; abased.

CONSTANCY = Fixedness; standing firm; firmness of mind.

FEARLESS = Freedom from fear.

IMPENDING = Hanging over; approaching near; threatening; about to happen.

DESTRUCTION = The act of destroying; demolition; pulling down; Death, Murder, Massacre.

WHEN WE GET GOD RIGHT, CULTURE FOLLOWS

I was just reading an article about a 12-year-old boy who took his life, because he was being bullied in school.

I WANT TO SAY THIS:

We, beyond a shadow of a doubt, need Jehovah God back into our schools and into our country. When we took God out of our schools (which is light), we allowed the enemy (which is darkness) to enter.

As I heard one wise man say, if we don't get God right in this next election, nothing else will matter. When we get God right, culture follows. We MUST put God back into our culture.

When the righteous are in POWER (and GOVERNING), the people
rejoice. When the wicked are in power, the people mourn. (Psalm
29:2)

Haven't so many been in mourning, in a greater measure, these last few years? I want to encourage us all to turn to the light, which is Jesus Christ, and continue daily to walk in that light. It is such a POWERFUL, PEACEFUL, ASSURING, ENCOURAGING, and FEARLESS place to live. From that place, we will be given strategies, answers, and solutions that we will not find anywhere else. It is VITAL that we work hard, diligently, wisely, and smart as we follow the strategies that are given to us.

I truly believe that the darkness that we are seeing all around us, is being eradicated and will continue to be eradicated by the light that is on the inside of us.

Let's continue to pray and intercede for each other, our great state, our country, and our world.

WE ARE MORE POWERFUL THAN WE REALIZE.

Love you ALL to life!

DEFINITIONS:

BULLY = A noisy, blustering overbearing fellow, more distinguished for insolence and empty menaces, than for courage, and disposed to provoke quarrels. A person who habitually seeks to harm or intimidate those whom they perceive as vulnerable.

CULTURE = The application of labor or other means to improve good qualities in, or growth; Any labor or means employed for improvement, correction, and growth.

GOVERNING = Having the authority to conduct the policy, actions, and affairs of a state, organization, or people.

REJOICE = To experience joy and gladness to a high degree; to exhilarate with lively and pleasurable sensations.

MOURN = To feel regret or sadness about the loss or disappearance of something.

ENCOURAGE = To give courage to; to give or increase the confidence of success; to embolden; to inspire with courage, spirit, or strength of mind.

ENCOURAGING = Inspiring with hope and confidence, exciting courage.

POWERFUL = Having a great moral power; forcible to persuade or convince the mind; efficacious.

PEACEFUL = Quiet; undisturbed; not in a state of war or commotion; removed from noise or tumult.

ASSURING = Making sure or confident, giving security, confirming.

FEAR = A painful emotion or passion excited by an expectation of evil or impending danger; anxiety.

FEARLESS = Free from fear; bold; courageous; Intrepid; undaunted.

STRATEGIES = A plan of action or policy designed to achieve a major or overall aim.

ANSWERS = A thing said, written, or done to deal with or as a reaction to a question, statement, or situation; to act in return.

SOLUTIONS = Resolution; explanation; the act of explaining or removing difficulty or doubt; release; deliverance; discharge. A means of solving a problem or dealing with difficult situations.

VITAL = Pertaining to life; being that which life depends; very necessary; highly important; essential.

HARD = Diligently; laboriously; importunately; with pressure; with urgency.

DILIGENTLY = With steady application and care; not negligently.

WISELY = Prudently; judiciously, discretely; with wisdom.

SMART = Having a quick-witted intelligence. Quick; pungent; vigorous.

ERADICATED = To destroy completely; to put an end to. To shoot as rays of light; to beam.

INTERCEDE = To intervene on behalf of another; to make intercession; to act between parties with a view to reconcile those who differ or contend; to plead in favor of one.

CHOOSING A LEADER IN ANY AREA OF GOVERNMENT

As I travel across the GREAT state of Michigan and around our country, I am often asked, "How do we choose the right candidate "?

As I was awakening one morning, I heard the words that I wrote in my article below.

The word of God gives us GREAT directions and is always a powerful resource. Please feel free to copy the article and share it with your friends, family, and community.

CHOOSING A LEADER IN ANY AREA OF GOVERNMENT:

First, look for a person of wisdom, one who understands and can discern the time and season that we are living in and are facing today. (Choosing a person of wisdom is key)

A person of wisdom will speak excellent and princely things. A person of wisdom will speak TRUTH and wrongdoing is detestable to them. (Proverbs 8:6-8)

Wisdom is the principle thing. (Proverbs 4:7) When we have wisdom, we have life and light.

For wisdom is better than rubies, and all the things one may desire cannot be compared with her. (Proverbs 8:11)

Wisdom dwells with prudence and finds out knowledge and discretion. (Proverbs 8:12)

Wisdom has counsel and sound knowledge. (Proverbs 8:14)

Wisdom has understanding, might, and power. (Proverbs 24:5)

By wisdom kings reign and rulers decree justice. (Daniel 2:21)

By wisdom princes rule and nobles, even all the judges and governors of the earth. (Proverbs 8:15-16)

A TRUE and GREAT leader does not have to be an expert in every field of governing, but they should have the ability, wisdom, and discernment to choose and place people in their administration who have the expertise and knowledge in the areas needed.

Look for a leader that will UPHOLD our United States CONSTITUTION and values. The U.S. was founded on Judeo-Christian values. That is what made our country great and prosperous. If we remove these values, which are our foundation, we are removing the light from our country; and if the light is removed, then darkness fills it.

We MUST NOT allow darkness to take over our country.

Look for a leader of character, one who cannot be bought with money, etc., and one who will not try to buy others with their wealth, etc.

Look for:

- A leader that is humble.

- A leader that genuinely loves all people

- A leader that can work well with all people

- A leader that is not a divider

- A fearless leader, one who will not capitulate and give in when threats and accusations come their way.

- A leader that is willing to bring UNITY and not division; although when doing the right thing may cause a separation, there is not a divisive motive behind it or attached to it.

A leader that understands the importance of how they deliver the truth. One may have the truth, but the delivery of that truth is vital. If we deliver the truth in a wrong manner, the truth may not be received.

It is VITAL that we RISE UP and take back our country.

Love you ALL to life!

DEFINITIONS:

WISDOM = The right use or exercise of knowledge; the quality of having experience, knowledge, and good judgment.

GOVERNING = Having the authority to conduct the policy, actions, and affairs of a state, organization, or people.

EXCELLENT = Being of great value or use, applied to things. Being of great virtue or worth.

PRINCELY = In a prince-like manner; of or held by a prince.

DETESTABLE = Extremely hateful; abominable

TRUTH = Conformity to fact or reality; the quality or state of being true. God's word is truth (St. John 17:17)

REIGN = The time during which a king, queen, or emperor possesses the supreme authority

DECREE = Judicial decision, or determination of a litigated cause.

JUSTICE = Practical conformity to the laws and to principles of rectitude in the dealings of men with each other; Impartiality.

KING = The chief or sovereign of a nation; a man invested with supreme authority over a nation, tribe, or country.

PRINCE = A sovereign; The chief and independent ruler of a nation or state.

RULE = Government; sway; empire; supreme command or authority.

DISCERN = To separate by the understanding, perceive, recognize; To see the difference between two or more things; To distinguish by the eye.

PRUDENCE = The ability to govern and discipline oneself by the use of reason; skill and good judgment; wisdom applied to practice.

KNOWLEDGE = A clear and certain perception of that which exists, or of truth and fact.

DISCRETION = Prudence; knowledge; that discernment which enables a person to judge critically of what is correct and proper, United with caution.

COUNSEL = Advice, opinion, or instruction is given up-on request or otherwise, for directing the judgment or conduct of another.

UNDERSTANDING = Comprehending; apprehending the ideas or sense of another, learning or being informed.

MIGHT = Strength; force; power.

POWER = Force, strength, energy.

NOBLES = A person of rank above a commander; a person of honorable family or distinguished by station.

JUDGE = A civil officer who is invested with authority to hear and determine causes, civil or criminal, between parties.

GOVERNOR = He that governs, rules, or directs, delegated authority. The elected executive head of a state of the U.S.

EXPERT = Properly, experienced; taught by use, practice, or experience, skillful, well instructed, having familiar knowledge of.

ADMINISTRATION = The act of administering; directing; management; government of public affairs; the conducting of any office or employment.

PRINCIPAL = Chief; highest in rank, character, or respectability; most important or considerable.

FOUNDATION = The basis or ground-working, of anything; that which anything stands, and by which it is supported; establishment.

CAPITULATE = To surrender, as an army or garrison, to an enemy.

VALUES = To rate at a high price; to consider with respect to importance; to estimate the worth of; a person's principles or standard of behavior.

THE LORD IS WITH YOU

This verse came to me early this morning:

Say to those who are fearful-hearted, "BE STRONG, do not fear!
Behold, your God will come with VENGEANCE and with the
RECOMPENSE of God; He will come and SAVE you".
(Isaiah 35:4)

The Lord wants you to live in His PEACE and not in the enemy's fear!

Be anxious for nothing, but in everything by prayer and supplication,
with thanksgiving, let your requests be made known to God; and the
peace of God, which surpasses all understanding, will guard your
hearts and minds through Christ Jesus. (Philippians 4:6-7)

The Lord, our precious Heavenly Father is ALWAYS on hand to
help you through whatever it is that is trying to bring fear, torment,
or anxiety upon you. He will never leave you nor forsake you.
(Deuteronomy 31:6).

The Lord has NOT left this country and The Lord has NOT left you.

Love you ALL to life!

DEFINITIONS:

FEARFUL-HEARTED = Feeling afraid, timid, anxious, or easily scared. Feeling overwhelmed; lacking courage or resolution.

FEAR = A painful emotion or passion excited by an expectation of evil, or the apprehension of impending danger; anxiety.

STRONG = Having the ability to bear or endure; firm, solid; well-fortified; able to sustain attacks; not easily subdued or taken.

VENGEANCE = The infliction of pain on another, in return for an injury or wrong.

SAVE = To preserve from injury, destruction, or evil of any kind. To rescue from danger.

RECOMPENSE = To compensate, to make a return of an equivalent for anything given, done or suffered; to require; to repay.

PEACE = A state of quiet or tranquility; freedom from disturbance or agitation; freedom from war.

GIVE THANKS

Today is another amazing and good day to give thanks and praise unto our Heavenly Father (our creator and maker of Heaven and Earth).

As we celebrate this beautiful day with family and friends or even by ourselves, let us offer up praises and THANKSGIVING to our Heavenly Father.

Let us not allow the stresses and trials in this life to steal our praise, joy, and THANKSGIVING unto the Lord. Let's on purpose be joyful, because the *JOY OF THE LORD IS OUR STRENGTH (Nehemiah 8:10)*.

Let's be thankful in everything. The Word admonishes us to rejoice in the Lord and to be anxious for nothing. It states in Philippians 4:6-7: *Be anxious for nothing, but IN EVERYTHING by prayer, supplication and THANKSGIVING let your requests be made known unto Him, and then the PEACE of God which surpasses ALL of our understanding, Will GUARD our hearts and mind through Christ Jesus.* I want us to notice that it says to thank the Lord **IN EVERYTHING**, not for everything. For example, if sickness & disease attacks the body, we are not to thank Him for the sickness, because He did not bring the sickness or disease.

Every good and perfect gift comes from above (James 1:17).

The thief, which is the enemy, comes only but to steal, kill and destroy, but Jesus came that we may have a full life and to have it more abundantly (St. John 10:10).

We are to thank Him IN the sickness not for the sickness (praise and thank Him for our healing). If we are being weighed down by the enemy with oppression, depression, anxiety, fears, torment, or the trouble and cares of this world, we are to give God praise IN IT, NOT FOR IT. When we do this, we are promised to have the PEACE of God to mount guard over our thoughts and mind.

THANKSGIVING and PRAISE is such a powerful weapon against the spirit of darkness. Darkness tries to come against us to overtake us. It is VITAL that *we put on the garment of praise and thanksgiving for the spirit of heaviness (Isaiah 61:3)*. If you are under such physical attack where you cannot at that time physically praise and thank the Lord, I want to encourage you to just meditate and think on His goodness. Remember you are thanking God in the situation, not for it. As we thank and give praise to our Heavenly Father, the darkness of sickness, worry, anxiety, fear, depression, oppression, torment, etc., will have to leave. It must give way to the light of THANKSGIVING. I want us all to know, understand and remember why we are praising and giving thanks unto the Lord. We are praising and *giving thanks unto the Lord because He is GOOD and His LOVINGKINDNESS and TENDER MERCIES endures FOREVER towards us! (Psalms 136:1)*

So again, let us all take time out today and every day to give THANKS and PRAISE unto the Lord!

Love you All To life!

DEFINITIONS:

THANKSGIVING = The act of rendering thanks or expressing gratitude for favors or mercies; a public celebration of divine goodness.

PRAISE = To commend; to applaud; to express approbation of personal worth or actions; to extol in words or songs; to magnify; to glorify on account of perfection or excellent worth.

CELEBRATE = To praise; to extol; to give praise; to honor by marks of joy and respect.

JOY = A glorious and triumphant state; The passion or emotion excited by the acquisition or expectation of good; Joy is a delight of mind from the consideration of the present or assured approaching possession of a good

PEACE = Freedom from agitation or disturbance by the passions as from fear, terror, anger, anxiety or the like. The quietness of mind, tranquility, and calmness.

ADMONISH = To warn or notify of a fault; to reprove with mildness.

ANXIOUS = Greatly concerned or solicitous; respecting something future or unknown; being in painful suspense.

PRAYER = talking and communicating with our Heavenly Father; a solemn address to the supreme God consisting of adoration, or an expression of our sense of God's glorious perfection.

SUPPLICATION = Entreaty, humble and earnest prayer in worship (petition; earnest request.

GUARD = To secure against injury; loss or attack; to protect; to defend; to keep in safety.

OFFER = Literally to bring to or before; hence.

TRIALS = Difficult experiences and problems; Challenges we endure in life that test our faith, love, and hope.

REJOICE = To experience joy and gladness to a high degree; to be exhilarated with lively and pleasurable; to exult.

VITAL = Absolutely necessary or important; essential.

FOCUS ON WHAT UNITES US AND RISE ABOVE WHAT DIVIDES US

I am reminded of a saying that my mother always kept before me as a child growing up. She said, "Bernadette, a wise person should never argue with a fool, because if a person hears or looks upon the argument, they cannot tell which one is the fool". *Wisdom is divine and it comes from the Lord. Jesus is the power and wisdom of God (I Corinthians 1:18).* You see, we may have a lot of knowledge, but we need wisdom to know what to do with knowledge and how to apply the knowledge.

It is so VITAL that we FOCUS on the TRUTH and what UNITES us and RISE above what divides us.

Truth is light and remember that the LIGHT always dispels the darkness. *God is light and in Him there is no darkness (I John*

1:5) Remember also that our U.S. Constitution and the Republican Platform DERIVES from light. It is like cream, and the cream rises to the top.

I want to encourage everyone to stop inward fighting, stop name-calling, and stop diagnosing each other. Your diagnosis may be totally wrong. Let us focus on spreading the truth of the history of our country, let us focus on spreading the truth of our platform and the truth of our U.S. Constitution. The truth is also that the Republican Party is the abolitionist party. The enemy's focus is to continually create confusion among us. He *(the devil) is the author of confusion and God is the author of peace (I Corinthians 14:33).* The enemy knows that if he can keep confusion going on among us, he can steal our unity and defeat us all.

We are totally STRONGER TOGETHER when we rally around the truth.

Let us focus on the truth and put our energy and time into stopping the lies of the critical race theory movement and that America is a racist country movement. America is not a racist country, although we may have some racist people in our country. Let us focus on stopping the shedding of innocent blood (abortion). Let us focus on rescuing and saving our children. Let us stop voter fraud. We must fight together for election integrity in our country and our world.

WE ARE AT WAR!! Let's stand together against this evil.

Love you ALL to life!

DEFINITIONS:

ARGUE = To dispute; strife; exchange or express diverging or opposite views typically in a heated or angry way.

FOOL = One who is destitute of reason or the common powers of understanding; a person who acts absurdly; one who acts contrary to sound wisdom.

WISE = Having knowledge; having the power of discerning and judging correctly, or discriminating between what is true and what is false; between what is fit and proper, and what is improper.

WISDOM = The right use or exercise of knowledge; the choice of laudable ends, and of the best means to accomplish them.

DIVINE = Pertaining to the true God; as the divine nature; divine protection.

KNOWLEDGE = A clear and certain perception of that which exists, or of truth and fact.

VITAL = Very necessary; highly important; essential.

FOCUS = A central point; point of concentration.

UNITY = The state of being one; undivided; uniformity

UNIFIED = To be joined in an act; to concur; to grow together.

RISE = To move or pass upward in any manner; to ascend.

TRUTH = Conformity to fact or reality; God's word (John 17:17)

LIGHT = Illumination; The natural agent that stimulates sight and makes things visible; something that makes vision possible.

DERIVES = Obtain something from a special source; to draw from, as a regular course or channel. To draw or receive, as from a source or origin.

ENCOURAGE = To give courage; to give or increase the confidence of success; to inspire with courage, spirit, or strength of mind; to embolden.

DIAGNOSE = Investigation or analysis of the cause or nature of a condition, situation, or problem.

ABOLITIONIST = A person who sought to abolish slavery during the 19th century.

ENGAGE

The Father of American Education, Noah Webster, expressed the purpose of schools was meant for the advancement of the Christian faith: "In my view, the Christian religion is the most important and one of the first things in which all children, under a free government, ought to be instructed. No truth is more evident to my mind than that the Christian religion must be the basis of any government intended to secure the rights and privileges of a free people". Unfortunately, in time, a philosophical shift took place in America, and the biblical principles for education were slowly eroded and abandoned, with sad and tragic consequences that continue to unfold, John Dewy; known as "The Architect of Modern Education," said, "There is no God, and there is no soul, Hence, there are no needs for the props of traditional religion." Those props have been knocked away, and the loss of moral standards has opened the door to untold numbers of unwanted teen pregnancies, abortions, drug abuse, alcoholism, violence, and suicide.

If we believe that the Founders were correct in asserting that America would fail if it lost its religious foundation, it is primarily incumbent upon Christian believers to reaffirm and reclaim our Christian educational heritage with the same passion and commitment of the Founders. There are many ways and many levels at which to instigate change, but it begins with a willingness to become engaged in the battle. (Noah Webster-1828)

It is VITAL that we all become engaged in the battle that we are facing in our country today.

I want to especially ENCOURAGE and URGE all pastors to become engaged in this battle.

Whether we want to accept it or not, we are at WAR. We are at war for the soul of our country, we are at war for the souls of our babies, we are at war for the soul of our children, and we are at war for the soul of our physical lives.

We must STAND up against this tyrannical government and speak TRUTH and EXERCISE our God given AUTHORITY and our CONSTITUTIONAL rights. Evil knows that we have already won, but it's banking on our ignorance and unwillingness to RISE UP against it.

We MUST stop evil at its core and not let it prevail against us or our country.

Let us ALL engage in the fight that is before us.

We must fight this war in the spirit as well as in the natural, trusting in God's ability and power to bring us total victory, and He will (Ephesians 6:12-17).

We must OCCUPY until Jesus comes back (Luke 19:13 KJV)

Let's get UNIFIED and LOCK arms together around the truth!!! Who then will be able to stop our mighty moving force? The answer is: NOBODY.

Love you ALL To life!

DEFINITIONS:

ENGAGE = To enlist; to embark in an affair; to occupy; to attack in a contest; to participate.

BATTLE = A fight, or encounter between enemies or opposing armies; an engagement.

WAR = An opposition between nations or states, carried on by force; either for defense or for revenging insults & redressing wrongs for extension of commerce or acquisition of territory or for obtaining and establishing the superiority and dominion of one over the other.

TYRANNICAL = Exercising power in a cruel or arbitrary way.

AUTHORITY = Legal power, or a right to command or to act.

CONSTITUTIONAL = A Body of fundamental principles or established precedents according to which a state or other organization is Acknowledged to be governed. Relating to an established set of principles governing a state.

OCCUPY = To take possession; to keep in possession; to take up; to employ; to use.

URGE = To press; to push; to impel.

ENCOURAGE = To give courage to; to give or increase the confidence of success; to inspire with courage spirit, or strength of mind, to embolden.

IGNORANCE = Absence or destitution of knowledge.

UNWILLINGNESS = Loathness; disinclination; Reluctance; unwillingness to do something.

CORE = The heart or inner part of a thing.

PREVAIL = To gain victory or superiority; to gain advantage; to overcome.

ENCODED = Gradually destroyed.

ABANDONED = Wholly forsaken or deserted.

REAFFIRM = To affirm a second time.

AFFIRM = To assent positively; to tell with confidence; to declare the existence of something.

RECLAIM = To claim back; to demand; to have returned.

RISE = To move or pass upward in manner; to get up; to leave a place of sleep or rest; ascent; the act of rising.

RIGHT = Conformity to the Will of God or His laws; The perfect standard of truth and justice; That which is morally correct, just, or honorable.

LOCK = To Unite closely by mutual insertion.

UNIFIED = To make or become united, uniform, or whole.

UNITED = Joined together politically for a common purpose or by a common feeling.

KEEP THE FAITH

I will lift up my eyes to the hills from whence comes our help! Our help comes from the Lord, who made heaven and earth. He will not allow our foot to be moved, He who keeps us will never SLUMBER Behold, He who keeps Israel shall neither slumber nor sleep. The Lord is our KEEPER; The Lord is our SHADE at our right hand. The sun shall not smite us by day nor the moon by night. The Lord shall PRESERVE us from ALL EVIL; He shall PRESERVE our SOUL. The Lord shall preserve our going out and our coming in from this time forth, and even FOREVER. (Psalms 121)

I want to encourage us all that we have nothing to fear but we have everything GOOD to gain. Why? because our precious Heavenly Father is with us. He said that He will never leave us nor forsake us. The Lord has not forsaken the US nor has He forsaken our COUNTRY!!

Keep the FAITH, follow his instructions, and rest in His power and ability to bring us over into GREAT VICTORY!!

Love you ALL to life!

DEFINITIONS:

SLUMBER = To sleep lightly, to be in a state of negligence, sloth

KEEPER = One who keeps, one that holds or has possession of anything; one who has the care.

SHADE = Protection; shelter; to cover from injury; to screen.

PRESERVE = To keep or save from injury or destruction; to defend from evil; to save from decay; to keep in a sound state.

EVIL= Not with justice or propriety; injuriously; unfortunate; not well.

SOUL= The mind, will, and emotions; the part of man which enables him to think and reason; life.

FOREVERMORE = For an endless time.

WE ARE NOT WRESTLING WITH FLESH AND BLOOD

"We must be FREE not because we claim FREEDOM, but because we PRACTICE it!"
~William Faulkner

It is VITAL and, on our watch, that we see to it that our great nation, THE UNITED STATES OF AMERICA, remains a FREE and beautiful country.

We must PRAY and FIGHT for the soul of our nation.

I want us all to know and recognize that: *we are not wrestling with flesh and blood (contending only with physical opponents), but we are wrestling against the despotisms, against the powers, against the master spirits who are the world rulers of this present darkness, against the spirit forces of wickedness in the heavenly (supernatural) sphere. (Ephesians 6:12).*

The good news is that we were given authority over the evil spirit of darkness. LET US ARISE and take our rightful place and exercise our authority over the evil that we see taking place in our country.

Behold, I give you the authority to trample on serpents and scorpions, and over all the power of the enemy, and nothing shall by any means hurt you. (Luke 10:19)

It was for freedom that Christ set us free (completely liberating us); therefore, keep STANDING FIRM and do not be subject again to a yoke of slavery (which you once removed) (Galatians 5:1)

I want to encourage us ALL to stand firm and together, in truth, against this darkness! Then we will all stand together in VICTORY!!

Love you ALL to life!

DEFINITIONS:

FREE = Instituted by free people, or by consent or choice of those who are to be subjects and securing private rights and privileges by fixed laws and principles; not arbitrary or despotic; as a free constitution or government.

FREEDOM = A state of exemption from the power or control of another; Liberty; exemption from slavery. The power or right to act, speak or think as one wants without hindrance or restraints.

STANDING = Continuance; duration or existence.

FIRM = Not giving way; strongly felt and unlikely to change.

YOKE = To enslave; to bring into bondage; to confine.

VITAL = Absolutely necessary; highly important.

SOUL OF THE NATION = The collective souls of the citizens.

PRAY = To ask with earnestness or zeal, as for a favor, or for something desirable; to entreat; to supplicate.

FIGHT = To maintain a struggle for victory over enemies; to control within battles; to war against.

SLAVERY = Bondage; the state of the entire subjection of one person to the Will of another.

PRACTICE = To do or perform frequently, customarily, or habitually; to perform by a succession of acts.

DESPOTISM = Absolute power; authority unlimited and uncontrolled by men, constitution or laws, and depending alone on the will of the prince.

ARISE = To ascend, mount up or move to a higher place.

AUTHORITY = Legal power, or a right to command or to act.

THIS IS AMERICA–
THIS IS HEROISM

In the great State of Michigan, a white police officer pulled a black young man out of a burning car saving his life.

Color WAS NOT the factor!

HUMANITY was the factor!

SAVING a LIFE was the factor!

The LOVE for a fellow American was the factor!

The COMPASSION for a fellow American was the factor!

The police officer putting his LIFE on the line was the factor!

In our world, today, so many are trying to make everything about race. The race card is being pulled out on every hand and side. It seems like the purpose is to bring division and confusion among the different ethnic groups, especially black Americans versus white Americans. We are ALL Americans.

I am convinced that if one can bring division between people then it will be easier to control them ALL. This evil divisive spirit must be ERADICATED.

You see, it should NEVER EVER be about race, because there is ONLY one race and that is HUMAN RACE.

Our Heavenly Father has made from one blood every nation of men to dwell on all the face of the earth, and has determined their reappointed times and boundaries of their dwellings…. (Acts 17:26).

I am certain that there are many more stories similar to this one that have happened or are happening all over our great country.

Let's SEEK to find the good in EVERYONE and PROMOTE the good in them.

It is VITAL that we FOCUS on what UNITES us and RISE above what tries to divide us.

Love you ALL to life!

DEFINITIONS:

HUMANITY = The human race which includes everyone on earth, mankind collectively

LOVE= An intense feeling of deep affection

COMPASSION = A suffering with another; painful sympathy; concern for the misfortunes of another

RACE= The lineage of a family, or continued series of descendants from a parent who is called the stock; Adam and Eve

HEROISM = The qualities of a hero; great bravery; courage; Intrepidity

ERADICATED= Plucked up by the roots; Destroyed

VITAL= Absolutely necessary or important; Essential

FOCUS = Point of concentration; The center of interest or activity

SEEK= To go in search or quest of; To look for; Attempt to find

PROMOTE = To contribute to the growth; To prefer in rank or honor; To support or actively encourage

THE LORD IS OUR LIGHT

These verses were coming to me for about a week, and as I woke up this morning, it came to me again:

> *The Lord is our LIGHT and our SALVATION whom shall we fear or dread? The Lord is the REFUGE and STRONGHOLD of our life of whom shall we be afraid? when the wicked, even our enemies and our foes, come upon us to eat up our flesh, they stumble and fall. Though a host encamps against us, our heart shall not fear; though war arises against us, even then, in this will we be confident. One thing that we must desire of the Lord, and seek after, is that we dwell in His presence ALL the days of our lives and behold His beauty and inquire in His temple. For in the day of trouble, He Will hide us in His shelter; in the secret place of His tent will He hide us; He Will set us high upon a rock... (Psalms 27:1-5).*

I want to encourage you all not to fear or dread what the evil one is trying to bring upon you personally or upon our country. We were told not to fear or dread! Why were we told not to fear or dread? The answer is because the Lord is our LIGHT, our SALVATION, our REFUGE, and the STRONGHOLD of our life. He told us that in the day of trouble, which we see all around our world today, He will HIDE us in His SHELTER (in the secret place of His tent). If we are hidden in Christ, how can darkness and the evil one find us?

It is vitally important that we are educated with the knowledge and understanding of this TRUTH! We are destroyed many times because of the lack of knowledge (truth) or we reject the knowledge (truth). (Hosea 4:6)

The enemy wants to bring us all under the power of fear because he knows that fear paralyzes people, and therefore he can come in and steal, kill, and destroy.

Philippians 1:28 tells us not to be frightened or intimidated in ANYTHING *by our opponents and our adversaries, for such constancy and fearlessness will be a clear sign (proof and seal) to them of (their impending) destruction, but (a sure token and evidence) of our deliverance and salvation, and that from God.* Isn't this EXCITING NEWS?

So let us all be BOLD, FEARLESS, CONFIDENT, and EXCITED. Continue to RISE up in FAITH and do not shrink in fear and let's take back what the enemy has already stolen from us and our country.

Love you ALL to life!

DEFINITIONS:

LIGHT = God is light and in Him, there is no darkness; The natural agent that stimulates sight and makes things visible; support, deliverance, Joy

SALVATION = The act of saving; preservation from destruction, danger or great calamity; loss, ruin

DREAD = To be in great fear

FEAR = A painful emotion or passion excited by an expectation of evil, or the apprehension of impending danger

IMPENDING = Hanging over you; approaching near; threatening; It's about to happen

REFUGE = To shelter; to protect; to shelter or protect from danger or distress

STRONGHOLD = A fastness; a fort; a fortified place; a place of security; a place where a particular cause or belief is strongly defended or upheld

FOE = An enemy, one who entertains personal enmity, hatred, grudge or malice against another; an enemy in war; one who opposes anything in principle.

FELL = To knock down, to cut, to bring down

KNOWLEDGE = A clear and certain perception of that which exists, or of truth and fact; learning; illumination of mind; information; the power of knowing

AFRAID = Impressed with fear or apprehension

HOST= An army; a number of men embodied for war; any great number or multitude

WAR = Hostility; state of opposition or contest; the act of opposition; enmity; disposition to contention

TROUBLE = To agitate; to disturb; to perplex; to afflict; to grieve; to distress

SHELTER = That which covers or defends from injury or annoyance; the state of being covered and protected; security

HIDE= To lie concealed; to keep oneself out of view; to be withdrawn from sight

FRIGHTENED = To terrify; to scare; to alarm suddenly with danger; to shock suddenly with the approach of evil

ADVERSARIES = An enemy or foe; one who has enmity at heart

DELIVERANCE = Release from captivity, slavery, oppression or any restraint; rescue from danger or any evil

FALL = The act of dropping or descending from a higher to a lower place by gravity; death; destruction, overthrow, ruin, degradation

INTIMIDATED = Frighten or overawe someone, especially in order to make them do what one wants.

PARALYZE = Rendered unable to think or act normally, especially through panic or fear; to bring a system, place, or organization to a standstill by causing disruption or chaos

WISDOM

I was in an amazing historic bookstore. After engaging with the owner for a short time, he said to me "GIVE ME SOME WISDOM ". I looked at him and then began to search within me and listen for directions from the Lord. I heard these words from my spirit and then I began to speak them to him. I said to him, "Of making many books there is no end, and much study is a weariness of the flesh. All has been heard, the end of the matter is, fear God and keep His commandments, for this is the whole duty of man". He looked at me with tears in his eyes and said, "GIVE ME MORE WISDOM". I then began to share more as I was led by the Lord.

I would like to elaborate on this word. In the book of *books there is no end (So DO NOT believe everything you read), and much study is a weariness of the flesh. All has been heard; the end of the matter is this; fear God (Revere and worship Him, knowing that He is) and keep His commandments, for this is the whole of man (the full original PURPOSE of His creation, the object of God's Providence, the root of character, the foundation of ALL happiness, the adjustment to ALL inharmonious circumstances and conditions under the sun) and the WHOLE DUTY for EVERY man. For God shall bring every work into judgment, with every secret thing. Whether it is good or evil. (Ecclesiastes 12:12-14)*

- What is the full, original purpose of our being created?

- What is the object of God's Providence?

- What is the root of our character?

- What is the foundation of ALL our happiness?

- What is the adjustment to ALL of our inharmonious circumstances and conditions under the sun?

- What is the WHOLE DUTY for EVERY man?

The answers to all these questions are to fear and worship God and keep His commandment.

The word fear means to reverence and worship God. We are not to be afraid of Him. He does not want us to be afraid of Him. He is our precious Heavenly Father who loves each and EVERY ONE of us with an EVERLASTING LOVE.

The Lord has appeared of old to me, saying: "Yes, I have loved you with an everlasting love; Therefore with lovingkindness I have drawn you. (Jeremiah 31:3)

God admonished us to keep His commandment. All of His commandments are wrapped up in one word, and that one word is the commandment of LOVE.

> **This is My commandment, that you love one another as I have loved you. (St. John 15:12)**

You may then ask, "WHAT IS LOVE"? One of the best definitions for love that I have found is in I Corinthians 13:4-8 from the Amplified Classic Bible. It states:

> *Love endures long and is patient and kind; love never is envious nor boils over with jealousy, is not boastful or vainglorious, does not display itself haughtily. It is not conceited (arrogant and inflated with pride); it is not rude (unmannerly) and does not act unbecomingly. Love (God's love in us) does not insist on its own rights or its own way, for it is not self-seeking; it is not touchy or fretful or resentful; it takes NO ACCOUNT of the evil done to it (It pays NO attention to a SUFFERED WRONG). It does not rejoice at injustice and unrighteousness but rejoices when RIGHT and TRUTH prevail. Love bears up under anything and everything that comes, is ever ready to BELIEVE the BEST of EVERY PERSON, it's hopes are fadeless under all circumstances, and it ENDURES everything without WEAKENING. LOVE NEVER FAILS...*

So, as we go through life let us be reminded of our PRIMARY PURPOSE in life. Our primary purpose in life is to worship, reverence, and praise our creator and to keep His commandment (LOVE). Every other purpose for our lives, (be it the President of the United States, Governor, spiritual leader, garbage collector, doctor, lawyer, engineer, school teacher, professor, business owner, nurse, musician, artist, movie actor, etc.), should ALL STEM from our primary purpose.

The Love of God is shed abroad in our hearts by the Holy Spirit, and we can choose to love with that love. (Romans 5:5)

> *We were ALL created to live for the praise of our Heavenly Father's glory. (Ephesians 1:12)*

I want us to all know and understand that divine wisdom comes from our Heavenly Father and Christ is the wisdom of God.

> *"...but to those who are called, both Jews and Greeks, Christ the power of God and the wisdom of God. Because the foolishness of God is wiser than men, and the weakness of God is stronger than men. (I Corinthians 1:24-25)."*

As we all work on becoming intimate with Him through the reading of the Bible and through worship, reverence, and love, our lives will begin to be governed by His wisdom and we will truly begin to walk in our divine purpose in this life. Knowing WHY WE EXIST and KNOWING OUR PURPOSE is vital to our success and happiness in life.

I want to encourage us all to always revere, worship and keep God's commandments and we will ride on the high places of life with such peace, joy and contentment.

Love you ALL to life!

DEFINITIONS:

> WISDOM = The quality of having experience, knowledge, and good judgment; the right use or exercise of knowledge.

> WEARINESS = Extreme tiredness; fatigue; Reluctance.

PURPOSE = The reason for which something is done or created or for which something exists.

INHARMONIOUS = Not living in peace and friendship; not forming or contributing to a pleasing whole discordant, negative state of mind.

PROVIDENCE = The protective care of God or of nature as a spiritual power; timely preparation for future eventualities.

CHARACTER = The mental and moral qualities distinctive to an individual.

FOUNDATION = The basis or groundwork, of anything; that on which anything stands, and by which it is supported.

FEAR = The worship of God; Reverence; respect; due regard. to have reverential awe.

JUDGMENT = The ability to make considered decisions or come to sensible conclusions, A misfortune or Calamity.

REVERE = To feel deep respect or admiration for something; to show devoted deferential honor to.

PRIMARY = First in order of time; first in the dignity of importance; principal (of chief importance)

ELABORATE = To expand someth2ing in detail; to develop or present a theory, policy, or system.

STEM= A central part of something from which other parts can develop or grow, or which forms support; Originate in or be caused by.

ADMONISHED = Advised, warned, instructed, urged.

RESURRECTION

I was sitting in my living room one morning, meditating on the purpose and the power of Jesus' death and resurrection, then I began to write these truths that came to me from the Lord.

- We were ALL lost and defeated (eternally doomed). The first man Adam brought us ALL into sin and out of fellowship with God our creator. He did this by disobeying God's word and following the dictates of his flesh, BUT Jesus Christ (the second man Adam) paid the price of death to bring us ALL out of sin and back into fellowship and right standing with God, our creator. Although Jesus Christ paid this wonderful price for us, we must believe in Him and make Him the Lord of our lives to receive these benefits.

- The prophet Isaiah prophesied the purpose of Jesus' crucifixion. He said "Surely Jesus has borne our griefs (sicknesses, weaknesses and distresses) and carried our sorrows and pains (of punishments), yet we considered Him stricken, smitten and afflicted by God; But He was wounded for our transgressions, He was bruised for our guilt and iniquities. The chastisement for our peace was upon Him, and by His stripes, we are healed. (Isaiah 53:4-5). NOTE: Jesus was wounded for our transgressions (sins), iniquities, peace, our financial prosperity, and our healing. You can find the words of these prophecies fulfilled in Matthew 8:16-17 and I Peter 2:24. Also, the fulfillment of this prophecy is found in Matthew 27. It states "About the sixth to ninth hour there was darkness over all the land, and about the ninth hour Jesus cried out with a loud voice saying Eli, Eli lama Sabachtani? Which means, My God, My God why have you forsaken me? Some of those who stood there, when they heard that said, this man is calling for Elijah! Immediately one of them ran and took a sponge filled it with sour wine and put it on a reed and offered it to Him to drink. The rest said let him alone, let us see if Elijah will come to save Him". And Jesus cried out again with a loud voice and yielded up His spirit (He died).

- On the Sabbath, there was a great earthquake; for an angel of the Lord descended from heaven and came and rolled back the stone from the door and sat on it. His countenance was like lightning, and his clothing was as white as snow. The guards shook for fear of him and became like dead men, but the angel answered and said to the woman, DO NOT BE AFRAID, for I know that you seek Jesus who was crucified. He is not here, FOR HE has RISEN as He said. Come see the place where The Lord lay and go quickly and tell His disciples that He is RISEN from the dead and indeed He is going before you in Galilee, there you will find Him. When they saw Him they worshipped Him, but some doubted.

- Jesus came and spoke to them, saying "ALL AUTHORITY has been given to me in heaven and on earth. Go therefore and make disciples of ALL nations, baptizing them in the name of the Father, and of the Son, and of the Holy Spirit. Teaching them to observe all things that I have commanded you, and lo I am with you ALWAYS, even to the end of the age. (Matthew 28:1-6 & 17:20)

GOD IS ALWAYS WITH US!!!

Jesus gave ALL AUTHORITY and POWER to the church.

Jesus put ALL *things under His feet and gave him to be head over ALL things, to the church, which is His body, the fullness of Him, who fills all in all (Ephesians 1:22)*

So, what power did Jesus give us? He gave us *the power and authority to trample over ALL the power that the enemy possesses (Luke 10:19).*

The POWER and the PURPOSE of the CROSS and RESURRECTION is to take your authority and dominion that Jesus Christ paid for you through His precious shed blood and exercise this power to defeat ALL of the darkness, demons and evil spirits that are lurking on earth.

Also, keep in mind that *Jesus was manifested to DESTROY and UNDO the works of demons and evil spirits. (I. John 3:8).*

This is how we are going to defeat the demons and darkness in our COUNTRY and our GOVERNMENT.

So DO NOT FEAR, but RISE up in FAITH. Let's be or continue to be the light on this earth.

<u>The light IN us will destroy the darkness AROUND us.</u>

Love you ALL to life!

DEFINITIONS:

RESURRECTION = The rising again to life

RIGHT STANDING = Being in the right relationship with the Lord.

INIQUITIES = Gross injustice; wicked

WOUNDED = INJURED; hurt by

BRUISED = To crush by beating or pounding with an instrument not edged or pointed

TRANSGRESSIONS = SIN, An act that goes against a law or rule

AUTHORITY = Delegated power

DISCIPLE = A follower; To convert, to teach or train or bring up

PROPHESIED = Foretold; predicted

CHASTISEMENT = Correction, punishment, the pain inflicted for punishment and correction, either by stripes or otherwise

HEALING = Restoring to a sound state

HEALED = Restore to a sound state

GUILT = The fact of having committed a specified or implied offense or crime

REED = A tall, slender leaved plant of the grass family, which grows in water or marshy ground.

OBSERVE = To be attentive; To conform one's action or practice to something such as a law, rite or condition

LURKING = To lie in wait in a place of concealment especially for an evil purpose; To persist in staying; To move furtively or inconspicuously; To concealed but capable of being discovered

ALIGNMENT

I heard these words as I was awakening one morning:

"There is a New World Order coming, but it is MY ORDER, says the Lord. Things are coming into ALIGNMENT; things are being RESTORED the way I always intended for it to be."

- Our country is being **restored**.
- Our country's finances are being **restored**.
- Our families are being **restored**.
- Our souls are being **restored**.
- Our health is being **restored**.
- Our finances are being restored.

I want to encourage EVERYONE not to lose HEART, not to lose FAITH and not to lose HOPE. Great and Mighty things are on the Horizon.

The Lord will RESTORE or REPLACE for you the years that the locust has eaten...And you shall eat in plenty and be satisfied and praise the name of the Lord, your God, who has dealt wondrously with you. And my people shall never be put to shame... (Joel 2:25-26).

These are truly times to rejoice and be glad, not sad. Let us watch and see the salvation of our God!!!

Love you ALL to life!

DEFINITIONS:

ALIGNMENT = The proper positioning; the ground plan; state of adjustment of parts; a forming in line; an arrangement of groups or forces in relation to one another.

RESTORE = To bring back (a previous right, practice, custom, or situation) Reinstate; to return (someone or something) to a former condition, place, or position; to repair or renovate; to return to its original condition.

HORIZON = It is almost certainly going to happen or be done quite soon; the line that terminates the view, when extended on the surface of the earth... range of perception or experience something that might be attained.

SOULS = The spiritual, rational, and immortal substance in man, which distinguishes him from brutes. The part of man which enables him to think and reason, and which renders him a subject of moral government.

HEART = The seat of the affections and passions, as of love, joy, courage, and pleasure. The seat of understanding.

FAITH = Belief; The assent of the mind to the truth of what is declared by another, resting on his authority and veracity without other evidence.

HOPE= A desire for some good, accompanied by at least a slight expectation of obtaining it, or a belief that it is obtainable.

REPLACE = To put again in the former place.

BRUTES = A beast; any animal destitute of reason; all animals

NOW WHAT?

Many are saying: "NOW WHAT? It looks like darkness has won and we have been defeated!"

To some, it looks like the Lord has forsaken us! Well, HE MOST CERTAINLY HAS NOT!

I'm reminded of the prophet Daniel. Daniel had an EXCELLENT spirit, and the king gave thought to set him over the whole realm of the kingdom. There were other leaders of the kingdom which consisted of all the governors, the administration, the satraps, the counselors, and the advisors, they were all very jealous of Daniel and began to plot against him to destroy him. Daniel was a praying man who prayed 3 times a day to the true and living God. The plot that the jealous and evil wicked leaders made against him was that they consulted together to establish a royal statute and to make a firm decree, that whoever petitioned any god or man for thirty days, except the king shall be cast into the den of lions. The king signed the writing. Daniel was not moved by what was done. He went home and with his windows open, prayed to his true and living God like he had before. When the evil and wicked leaders found Daniel praying, they told the king. The king's heart was broken because he loved Daniel, but because he signed the decree, he had to follow through with it. They cast Daniel into the den of lions.

It seemed like the evil; wicked and dark men had won! It seemed like darkness gained victory, but the Lord was with Daniel. The Lord shut the lion's mouths. The lions were unable to hurt Daniel. Because Daniel trusted in the Lord. Daniel was delivered from being eaten up by the lions.

The evil and wicked men that plotted against Daniel to destroy him were brought before the king, and the king had those men thrown into the den of lions. The lions destroyed those men. (Daniel 6:1-28)

There have been many evil and wicked men that have plotted against our country for decades to destroy it. It seems like they have won. It seems like darkness has prevailed, BUT IT HAS NOT!! God is with us like he was with Daniel.

DO NOT EVER ALLOW TIME TO DETERMINE DEFEAT!

We have already won!

Just like our God shut the lieon's mouth for Daniel, He will shut the mouths of those that speak lies against President Trump our COUNTRY, and you.

But the king shall rejoice in God;Everyone who swears by Him shall glory; But the mouth of those who speak lies shall be stopped. (Psalms 63:11)

THE LORD KNOWS WHAT'S IN THE DARKNESS, AND LIGHT DWELLS WITH HIM!! (Daniel 2:22)

I want to encourage you all to keep dwelling in the light by worshipping and praising our true and living God and you will see the VICTORY MANIFESTED!!

Please remember: DO NOT ALLOW TIME TO DETERMINE DEFEAT!!

The Egyptians you see today, you will not see again (Exodus 14:13)

Love you ALL To life!

DEFINITIONS:

MANIFESTED = Made clear; disclosed; made apparent; obvious or evident

EXCELLENT = Being of great virtue or worth being of great value or use.

SATRAPS = An admiral; more generally, the governor of a province.

DECREE = Judicial decision or determination of a litigated cause.

PETITION = A request, supplication, or prayer.

STAND

Keep the FAITH, stand FIRM, and stand STILL. DO NOT BE AFRAID. Watch and see the SALVATION of the Lord, which He will ACCOMPLISH for our country!!!

Our country was founded on Judeo-Christian values!!!

*I want to encourage you all to read Exodus 14 *take notice of verse 13: And Moses said to the people, "Do not be afraid. Stand still, and see the salvation of the Lord, which He will accomplish for you today. For the Egyptians whom you see today, you shall see again no more forever.*

The Red Sea will be departed in our country and in our lives.

Love you ALL to life!

DEFINITIONS:

FAITH = A firm, cordial belief in the veracity of God, in all the declarations of his word. Complete trust or confidence in someone or something.

FIRM = To settle; Not easily moved, steady, unshaken, stable.

STAND STILL = Remain calm, remain in place, remain fixed or immobile.

AFRAID = Impressed with fear, feeling fear or anxiety, frightened, worried.

SALVATION = The act of saving; preservation from destruction, danger, or great calamity.

ACCOMPLISH = To execute, to bring to pass, achieve or complete successfully, to carry out or finish an action, to complete what you set out to do, to fulfill.

CHRISTIANITY IS NOT A DENOMINATION

Benjamin Rush, a signer of the Declaration of Independence, wrote in a letter to Thomas Jefferson:

"I have always considered Christianity as the strong ground of republicanism. The spirit is opposed, not only to the splendor, but even to the very forms of monarchy, and many of its precepts have for their object republican liberty and equality as well as simplicity, integrity, and economy in government. It is only necessary for republicanism to ally itself with the Christian religion to overturn ALL the corrupted political and religious institutions in the world."

> *While they promise them liberty, they themselves are slaves*
> *of corruption; for by whom a person is overcome, by him also he is*
> *brought into bondage. (II Peter 2:19)*

I want to encourage and urge all pastors, all teachers, all leaders, all Christians, and ALL people to educate and continue to educate the truths of these words.

Christianity IS NOT a DENOMINATION, but it is the Kingdom of God! (Christ taught the kingdom of God) *But seek first the kingdom of God and His righteousness, and all these things shall be added to you. (Matthew 6:33)*

Love you ALL To life!

DEFINITIONS:

CHRISTIANITY = The system of doctrines and precepts taught by Christ.

CHRISTIAN = A believer and follower of Christ.

EDUCATE = To inform and enlighten the understanding.

THE FINGER OF GOD

Yesterday morning I heard these words from my spirit:

"THE FINGER OF GOD"

I am reminded of when Pharaoh, (who was the head of the government and the religious leader in Egypt), brought the children of Israel under Great Depression, Great Hardship and Great Bondage.

...One day because of the wickedness of Pharaoh towards the children of Israel, the Lord spoke to Moses and told him to tell Aaron, (his brother) to stretch out his rod and strike the dust of the land so that it becomes lice throughout all the land of Egypt. Aaron obeyed the Lord and lice flooded the land of Egypt. Pharaoh's magicians (the enemy) tried to copy Aaron, by attempting to bring lice throughout the land by their enchantments, but they could not. Then the magicians said to Pharaoh, "THIS IS THE FINGER OF GOD" (Exodus 8:16-19)

The finger of God is the Spirit of God.

Matthew 12:27-28: And if I cast out demons by Beelzebub, by whom do your sons cast them out? Therefore, they shall be your judges. But if I cast out demons by the Spirit of God, surely the kingdom of God has come upon you.

Luke 11:20: But if I cast out demons with the finger of God, surely the kingdom of God has come upon you.

One touch of God's finger upon the wickedness of our country, will totally destroy, eradicate and dissipate ALL of the enemy's agendas, plots, and schemes against our country and also that are against you.

I want to encourage ALL of you to be STRONG and COURAGEOUS! Do not be afraid or terrified because of them, for the Lord your God goes with you, He will never ever leave you nor abandon you. (Deuteronomy 31:6)

The Lord will be with you wherever you GO!! You are safe and secure with Him!

Love you ALL to life!

DEFINITIONS:

ENCHANTMENTS = Demonic powers; The state of being under a spell; Magic

DESTROY = Demolish; to pull down

ERADICATE = To pull up the roots; to destroy thoroughly

DISSIPATE = To scatter; to drive asunder; vapor

STRONG = Well fortified; able to sustain attacks and pressure; having a great force of mind and intellect

COURAGEOUS = Brave; Bold; to hardy to encounter difficulties and dangers

AFRAID = Impressed with fear or apprehension

TERRIFIED = Frightened; cause to feel extreme fear

ABANDON = One who totally forsakes or deserts

WE ARE FREE

In 1843, Emma Willard, a historian, and pioneer who founded the first women's school of higher education, wrote: "The government of the United States is acknowledged by the wise and good of other nations, to be the most FREE, IMPARTIAL, and RIGHTEOUS government of the world; but all agree, that for such a government to be SUSTAINED for many years, the principles of TRUTH and RIGHTEOUSNESS taught in the Holy Scriptures, must be practiced. The rulers must govern in the fear of God, and the people obey the laws "

I encourage all spiritual leaders and ALL leaders to RISE up or continue to RISE up and educate and demonstrate to others this TRUTH!!

In Jesus' Name, the United States of America will remain a FREE, IMPARTIAL, and RIGHTEOUS government.

The enemy WILL NOT steal this election and he WILL NOT steal this country!!!

Love you ALL to life!

DEFINITIONS:

FREE = Not enslaved; not in a state of vassalage or dependence

IMPARTIAL = Not partial; not biased; unprejudiced

RIGHTEOUS = Just; accordant to divine law

RIGHTEOUSNESS = Purity of heart and rectitude of life;

the quality of being morally right or justifiable

SUSTAINED = Upheld; maintained; to keep from falling; to keep from sinking

TRUTH = Conformity to fact or reality; God's word (John 17:17)

Love you All to life!

DEFINITIONS:

TYRANNICAL = Exercising power in a cruel or arbitrary way; oppressive and controlling.

CIVIL UNREST = Acts of violence and disorder detrimental to the public law and order; Riots etc.

INTERCEDE = Intervene on behalf of another; You plead in favor of one.

SHENANIGANS = Secret or dishonest activity or maneuvering.

INTERCEDE

I heard out of my spirit these words:

"Will the just judge of all the world do right?"

I was immediately reminded of the story of how Abraham interceded for the city of Sodom:

> There was a great outcry against the cities of Sodom and Gomorrah, because of the greatness of their sin. Abraham's nephew, Lot, and his family, lived in Sodom. Lot was a righteous man. The wickedness of Sodom became so exceedingly great, that destruction was determined against them. Abraham began to intercede for Sodom. He asked the Lord this question, "Lord, would you destroy the righteous with the wicked?" Suppose there were fifty righteous within the city; would you also destroy the place and not spare it for the fifty righteous that are in it?" Abraham went on to say "Far be it from you Lord! SHALL NOT THE JUDGE OF ALL THE EARTH DO RIGHT?" The Lord responded back to Abraham and said "If I find in Sodom fifty righteous within the city, then I will spare all the place for the fifty sakes." Then Abraham asked the Lord, would you save the city of Sodom for 45, for 40, for 30, for

20, and even for 10 righteous? *The Lord responded back again to him and said "Abraham if I find only 10 righteous people in Sodom, I will not destroy it. (Genesis 18:1-32)*

I can't help but see the goodness and mercies of our Heavenly Father upon the city of Sodom. We truly serve an amazing and good father.

Now let's take a look at the United States of America! There has been so much evil and wickedness that has happened and still happening in our country. For example, all of the civil unrest, all of the abortions, all of the human trafficking, and ALL of the other SHENANIGANS that are happening; but

I truly believe, just like the Lord was willing to spare the city of Sodom if He could find only 10 righteous people in that city that He is willing to spare the United States from a TYRANNICAL GOVERNMENT.

Let us continue to INTERCEDE for our country like Abraham interceded for Sodom and watch our Heavenly Father spare and save our country.

The just GOD of ALL the earth will do right!!

Love you ALL to life!

DEFINITIONS:

TYRANNICAL = Exercising power in a cruel or arbitrary way; oppressive and controlling.

CIVIL UNREST = Acts of violence and disorder detrimental to the public law and order; Riots etc.

INTERCEDE = Intervene on behalf of another; You plead in favor of one.

SHENANIGANS = Secret or dishonest activity or maneuvering.

IT IS NOT OVER

The word of the Lord came to me saying,

"The sword of the Lord and Gideon".

As I began to read and meditate on this saying, *"The sword of the Lord and Gideon"*, this is what came to me: *The children of Israel were greatly impoverished and oppressed by the Midianites for 7 years. They then began to cry out to the Lord. The Lord heard their cry and sent a prophet to encourage them. The prophet reminded them of how their God had delivered them in the past. The prophet told them not to fear the gods of the Amorites. (Israel's disobedience brought them into captivity with the Midianites).*

The angel of the Lord also appeared to Gideon and said to him, "The Lord is with you, you mighty man of valor!" Gideon said to the Lord, "Oh my Lord if you are with us, why then has all this happened to us? It truly seemed like the Lord had forsaken Israel. Then the Lord told Gideon that He was with him and that he would use him to save Israel from the hand of the Midianites. The Lord told Gideon to tear down the altar of Baal (an Idol) and cut down the wooden image that was beside it. He reassured Gideon that he was with him and that the Midianites would be defeated through him. Gideon obeyed the Lord and tore down Baal and cut down the wooden image that was beside it. The Midianites, Amalekites, and the people of the East were very angry, and they gathered together to destroy Gideon and the children of Israel. The Midianites, Amalekites, and the people of the East were great in number (as numerous as locusts) and Gideon ONLY had 300 men with him (so that Israel could not claim glory for itself against God); but the Lord gave Gideon the plan and strategy on how to defeat his enemies. Gideon followed and obeyed the plan and the strategy that the Lord gave to him; in which he totally destroyed and eradicated his enemies (The Midianites, Amalekites, and all the people of the East). (Judges 6 & 7)

Many people are feeling today the same way that Gideon and the children of Israel felt. Many are feeling OPPRESSED by FACTIONS in our government. You may be asking, Lord if you are with us, why is this all happening in our 2020 Election and in our country? It may seem like the Lord has forgotten us. Liken the Midianites to what we are facing in our 2020 Election and our country today. The Midianites can be compared to the swamp. It appears that they have won and that everything is over for our President and our country. Note the word:

APPEARS! THINGS ARE NOT ALWAYS AS THEY APPEAR.

The Lord is with our country like He was with Gideon and the children of Israel. The righteous leaders were sent to the American People. They are sent to drain the swamp (the leftist wicked agenda).

The swamp is so angry at the accomplishments of our president, which include exposing the corruption and bringing down the leftist wicked agenda. The leftists are pulling out every dark force in their arsenal against the President's Administration, just like the Midianites and Amalekites did against Gideon.

It's NOT over!! WAKE UP and SHOUT the VICTORY you mighty men and women of valor!!! For the Lord, our God is with US like He was with Gideon.

Expect to see MANIFESTED VICTORY!!!!

Keep the faith, keep praying, keep praising, and keep standing strong against this evil darkness that surrounds us. YOU are LIGHT (if you accepted Jesus as your Lord and savior) and light will overpower, destroy and eradicate the darkness.

Love you ALL to life!

DEFINITIONS:

FACTIONS = A small, organized dissenting group within a large one, especially in politics.

APPEAR = To come or be in sight; give the impression of being

LEFTIST = A person with left-wing political views

OPPRESSED = Subject to harsh and authoritarian treatment

BENEFIT PACKAGE

I sat down after my prayer time with my Heavenly Father and I began to meditate on these words:

> *Bless the Lord oh my soul and ALL that is within me bless His holy name. (Psalms 103:1)*

Then the Lord began to reveal and break down in part these verses to me. Our soul is our mind, our will, and our emotions.

To **BLESS** the Lord is to PRAISE and to GLORIFY for benefits received.

To **GLORIFY** is to praise; magnify and honor in worship; to ascribe honor to in thought or words.

> *Psalms 86:9 states: ALL nations whom you have made shall come and worship before you oh Lord and shall glorify your name.*

> *Then Psalms 103:2 goes on to say: Bless the Lord oh my soul and forget not ALL HIS BENEFITS.*

A benefit is an act of kindness; a favor conferred; expressing whatever contributes to promoting prosperity and personal happiness or adding value to property.

I want to share with you some of our Heavenly Father's **AMAZING** benefits that He has given to us.

1. HE FORGIVES ALL OF YOUR INIQUITIES:

An iniquity is a sin or crime, wickedness, or any act of injustice. A habitual habit of sin; a premeditated choice.

Therefore, through one man's offense judgment came to all men, resulting in condemnation, even so through one Man's righteous act the free gift came to all men, resulting in justification of LIFE (Romans 5:18) This awesome benefit does not license us to sin. Sin opens up the door for the devil to steal from us. So, you do not want to sin ok? Paul says it this way, shall we continue in sin that grace May abound? The answer is CERTAINLY NOT, but should you sin, know that you are forgiven. This is one of your benefits. Knowing that you are forgiven should give you the desire to please our Heavenly Father that much more. It should give you the desire to become intimate or more intimate with Him.

2. HE HEALS ALL YOUR DISEASES:

Disease is to interrupt or impair any or all the natural and regular functions of the several organs of a living body; to interrupt or render imperfect the regular functions of the brain, or of the intellect; to pain to make uneasy. We have all been redeemed from sickness by the precious blood of Jesus. Jesus bore it for us.

(Isaiah 53:4-5, Matthew 8:17, I Peter 2.24)

3. HE REDEEMED YOUR LIFE FROM DESTRUCTION:

Destruction is the action or process of causing so much damage to something that it no longer exists or cannot be repaired. You may feel like there is no way that this attack on your finances, your mind, your body, your family, and this country can be repaired, but I want you to know that You have been redeemed from it. It is part of your benefit package. Take it. It's yours. You will see your destruction repaired. We will also see our country repaired and restored!

4. HE CROWNED YOU WITH LOVING KINDNESS AND TENDER MERCIES:

To crown is to honor; to dignify; to adorn; to reward; to recompense. Loving-Kindness is tender, regard, mercy, and favor. Mercy is compassion or forgiveness shown toward someone whom it is within one's power to punish or harm.

The word of the Lord also states that He will not take away His loving kindness from you nor will He allow His faithfulness to fail. His Covenant He will not break, nor alter the words that have gone out from His lips (Psalms 89:33)

We are so crowned with the loving kindness, favor, and mercies from our Heavenly Father. Let's make and keep Him the center of our lives.

5. HE SATISFIES YOUR MOUTH WITH GOOD THINGS:

To satisfy is to free from doubt; suspense or uncertainty; to cause the mind to rest in confidence by ascertaining the TRUTH; to supply possession or enjoyment till no more is desired. You ascertain the truth by reading, studying, and applying the word to your life. *God's word is truth (St. John 17:17).* Our Heavenly Father satisfies us with good things. He does not satisfy us with bad things, He does not satisfy us with tormenting thoughts of worry, fear, or anxiety. He does not satisfy us with sickness and disease., He does not satisfy us with the lack of anything. He satisfies us with peace, joy, health, wealth, and happiness. He satisfies us with a blessed marriage, He satisfies us with blessed children, and He satisfies us with blessed friendships. He satisfies us with the riches of His glory. He satisfies us with everything good.

6. HE RENEWS OUR YOUTH LIKE THE EAGLES:

To renew is to be made new again; to restore to a former state, or to a good state after decay or deprivation; to rebuild, to repair; to begin again. When we look to Jesus and follow what he says He will make all things new for us. You will become strong, overcome, and soaring. Jesus told us to *look away from all that would distract us and look to Him for He is the author and finisher of our faith (Hebrews 12.3).*

Many of you know what's in your earthly employee benefits package. How much more should we know about what's in our benefits package from our Heavenly Father?

I want to encourage everyone to BLESS the Lord for He is truly good and so worthy of ALL of our praises.

Take full possession of your BENEFIT package. It belongs to you.

Love you ALL to life!

TAKING THE LIMITS OFF GOD

As I was leading a prayer meeting at our church, I saw and heard these words:

"Tell my people to take the limits off of me." I am God, their creator, and maker of heaven and earth. (Psalms 146:6)

As there appears to be some SHENANIGANS going on regarding this election, God is still God. He is God today; He will be God tomorrow and forever. For God Himself has said ... *I will not in any way fail you nor give you up, nor leave you without support. I will not, I will not, I will not in any degree leave you helpless nor let you down! Assuredly Not!! So we take comfort and are encouraged and confidently and boldly say, The Lord is my helper; I will not fear or dread or be terrified. What can man do to me? (Hebrews 13:5-6 AMPC)*

Many are concerned about their future and the future of their children and their grandchildren. I hear the Lord saying, "Teach your children and grandchildren to get to know Him intimately by praying (talking to him), by reading the word of God (the Holy Bible), and by applying the word to their lives."

By doing this they will have a BLESSED and PROSPEROUS life. They will not be limited by the government or society. God is bound by His word. (Hebrews 6:17 NLT & Psalms 119:89). Do not fear because of the darkness that you see around us. Light will dispel ALL darkness.

Proverbs 3:5-6 (AMP) states: TRUST in and be CONFIDENT in the Lord with ALL your heart and mind and do not rely on your own insight or understanding. He said in ALL your ways know, recognize, and ACKNOWLEDGE Him and He will DIRECT and make straight and plain your paths. The word direct means moving from one place to another in the shortest way and showing the RIGHT ROAD OR COURSE. So we do not have to be concerned or worry about what the enemy is doing and all of the shenanigans that are going on around us. All we need is faith and confidence in our God and in His ability and power to perform on our behalf. He will lead and guide us and show us the way to escape and deliverance. He will never leave us nor forsake us. Do not be intimidated or fearful by what the enemy is trying to do.

Be ENCOURAGED and take the LIMITS off!!!

We win when we put our total trust and confidence in God!!

Love you ALL to life!

DEFINITIONS:

LIMIT = To confine within certain bounds

TRUST = Confidence; a reliance or resting of the mind on the integrity of another person

CONFIDENT = One entrusted with secrets

ACKNOWLEDGE = To own, avow or admit to being true

SHENANIGANS = Secret or dishonest activity or maneuvering

REVIVAL

Our country is in need of a REVIVAL!

A revival from the Holy Spirit will bring forth a great AWAKENING to America and our world.

This is a CRITICAL time. It is the hour for us to be AWAKENED from our sleep (of spiritual COMPLACENCY); for our salvation is nearer to us now than when we first believed (in Christ).

The night (This present evil age) is almost gone and the day (of Christ's return) is almost here. So let us FLING away the works of darkness and put on the full armor of LIGHT. (Romans 13:11-12)

As we put on the full armor of light (God's word), *We will then RISE from the depression, anxiety, confusion, and fear in which circumstances have kept us. We will RISE to a new life. We will be radiant with the GLORY of the Lord and His manifestation will be upon us. (Isaiah 60:1)*

When the MANIFESTATION and the AWAKENING of the Holy Spirit come upon us, ALL worry, fear, anxiety, confusion, and torment from the evil one will leave us. There will also be a mighty PARADIGM SHIFT in our personal lives and in our country. We will truly experience, for ourselves, the LIGHT dispelling the darkness in every area.

Every one of us is so LOVED by our Heavenly Father! Let us receive His love, OK?

Love you ALL to life!

DEFINITIONS:

REVIVAL = To recall, return or recover from a state of neglect, oblivion, obscurity or depression

AWAKEN = To rouse from sleep; to put into action or

new life

AWAKENING = An act or moment of becoming suddenly aware of something; coming into existence or awareness

FLING = Throw forcefully; to cast; to hurl

COMPLACENCY = Self-satisfaction; unaware or uninformed

MANIFEST = To make known; perceived by the senses.

MANIFESTATION = The act of disclosing what is secret, unseen or obscure

GLORY = Brightness, luster, splendor, magnificence

RISE = To ascend; to get up

WE WIN

This is the result of ALL of our (WORD based) prayers. Let us continue to praise our Heavenly Father for what He is accomplishing through and for our President.

I Timothy 2:1-3 states: Therefore I exhort FIRST of all those
supplications, prayers, intercessions, and giving of thanks be made for
ALL men, for kings and ALL who are in authority, that WE may lead
a QUIET and PEACEABLE life in ALL godliness and reverence. For
this is good and acceptable in the sight of God our Savior.

Isaiah 55:11 states: So shall my WORD be that goes forth from my
mouth; it shall not return to me void, But it shall ACCOMPLISH
what I please, And it shall PROSPER in the thing for which I sent it.

We win and REVIVAL is here!

Love you ALL to life!

DEFINITIONS:

ACCOMPLISH = To finish entirely; to complete successfully; To fulfill to bring to pass.

PROSPER= To be successful; to succeed, to thrive, To make a gain.

PRAYING FOR OUR PRESIDENT

It is such a GREAT privilege to pray and intercede for our President, President Donald J. Trump, and his precious, beautiful, and sweet wife Melania.

I pray to God Most High, who PERFORMS on President Trump's behalf and REWARDS him (who brings to pass His PURPOSES for him and surely COMPLETES them)! He will send from heaven and save him from slanders and reproaches of those who would trample him down or swallow him up (with their mouths and actions). The Lord will put them to shame. His life is among lions; he lies among those who are aflame-the sons of men whose teeth are spears and arrows and their tongues sharp swords. (Psalms 57:2-4)

I am convinced and sure of this very thing, that Our Heavenly Father has begun a good work in President Trump and He will continue His good work THROUGH him and IN him. (Philippians 1:6)

So many years ago, the enemy planned and plotted to bring down the United States. He truly thinks that he is winning, but there is one thing that the enemy did not factor in, and that is the ANOINTING. You see, one touch of the ANOINTING from our Heavenly Father upon the United States will ERADICATE and DISSIPATE all the plots, schemes, and plans of the enemy.

Be ENCOURAGED, keep the FAITH, and keep APPLYING the word of God over our President and over our GREAT country, The United States of America!!

We WIN!!!!!!

DEFINITIONS:

ANOINTING = Burden removing, yoke destroying the power of God!!

ERADICATE = To destroy thoroughly; to destroy anything that grows; to put an end to!!

DISSIPATE = To drive asunder; to scatter; to disperse, to separate Into parts and disappear.

CHOOSE LIFE

We have ALL missed it in life, but WE cannot afford to miss it regarding this election. I am reminded of this bible verse. It states: *Now listen!! Today I am giving you a choice between LIFE and DEATH, between PROSPERITY and DISASTER, between BLESSINGS and the CURSES; Oh that you would CHOOSE LIFE so that you and your descendants might LIVE. (Deuteronomy 30:19 NLT)*

This is a multiple-choice question, and we were given the correct answer. The answer is: CHOOSE LIFE!

When we CHOOSE candidates whose policies align with the word of God, we are CHOOSING LIFE, LIBERTY, and the PURSUIT of happiness!!

Join me in CHOOSING pro-Jehovah God, pro-Life, pro-America, and pro-the U.S. Constitution candidates!

Love you ALL to life!

WAY MAKER

The word of the Lord came to me saying:

"He will defend and protect and avenge His children speedily", however, when the Son of Man comes, will He find FAITH ON THE EARTH?" (Luke 18:8)

(Will He find us TRUSTING in Him when He returns?) The Lord said cursed (with great evil) is the strong man who trusts in and relies on frail man, making weak (human) flesh his arms. (Jeremiah 17:5)

Our Heavenly Father wants our TOTAL TRUST and DEPENDENCY to be ONLY in Him. He is our waymaker and the source of ALL things. (I Corinthians 8:6)

He has great and mighty plans for each and every one of us. We were all born with, and for, a divine purpose, in which we are given the opportunities to walk out in our lifetime.

For I know the thoughts that I think toward you, says the Lord,

thoughts of peace and not of evil, to give you a future and a hope.

(Jeremiah 29:11)

It does not matter how old you are, God's PLANS for your life still STANDS. As long as there is breath within you, you can still fulfill God's divine purposes and plans for your life.

The word of the Lord states in Philippians 1:6: For I am

CONVINCED and SURE of this very thing that He who began

a GOOD work in you will continue until the day of Jesus Christ

(right up to the time of His return) developing (that good work) and

perfecting and bringing it to full completion in us.

Our Heavenly Father needs our trust and dependency to be in Him in order for us to EFFECTIVELY walk out and fulfill His divine purpose in our lives.

FAITH is reading, believing, and then acting upon the words written in the Holy Bible.

Our faith will definitely be challenged by the evil one. I can assure you of this. You may even feel that you have hit rock bottom with no return. Remember this, if you are at the bottom, you can only rise up.

Our Lord told us how to handle the challenges of the evil one. He said for us to *look away from ALL that will DISTRACT us from JESUS, who is the leader, source, and finisher of our faith (bringing it to maturity and perfection) in us.* (Hebrews 12:2 AMPC)

So then let us look clear away from everything that opposes the written words of our Heavenly Father and clings to and stays FOCUSED only on His words. We must resist the evil one by believing and saying only what the word says about us. We will never be put to shame if we put our trust and dependency on Jesus (Romans 10:11).

Please know this: Heavenly Father works through men, for example, Doctors, Lawyers, Teachers, Mentors, Bosses, etc. BUT He wants our total trust and dependency to be upon Him. He will speak to and deal with men on our behalf. THIS IS FAITH!!

God knows how to fix every situation and circumstance that arise in our lives.

> *When our trust and dependency are on Him, He will lead us to the PERFECT JOB. He will lead us to the right doctor, the right church, the right school/ university, the right mate, etc. He said that He will show us things to come. When, He, the spirit of truth (the truth-giving Spirit) comes, He will guide us into ALL the truth (The whole full truth). For He will not speak His own message (On His own authority); but He will tell whatever He hears from the Father. He will tell us what will happen in the future. (St. John 16:13).*

Many may feel and believe that our Heavenly Father has forgotten them. I want to let you know this day that NO He has not forgotten you. *He said that He will NEVER EVER leave you nor FORSAKE you. (Deuteronomy 31:6)*

I want to also encourage us all, not to ever go by our feelings, but to ONLY go by, speak and stand on the Word of God.

> *Our Heavenly Father thinks GOOD thoughts about us. He said that His thoughts of us are more in number than the GRAINS of SANDS (Psalms 139:17-18).*

When Jesus hung on the cross, He knew us (all of our failures and shortcomings) yet He loved us and paid the ultimate sacrifice for mankind.

I would like to encourage everyone not to put our trust in mere men (the government etc., the mask, etc. as their protection and source, but to put our trust and dependency on their Heavenly Father, the maker of Heaven and Earth. In doing this, our road in life will be smoother and with greater peace, comfort, joy, and great VICTORY!!

Let us make this our confession: When Jesus comes back again, He will find FAITH IN ME!!

Love you ALL to life!

DEFINITIONS:

WAY MAKER = One that makes a road specifically

PURPOSE = To intend; to design, that which a person sets before himself as an object to be reached or accomplished.

DISTRACT = To draw apart; to pull in different directions and separate.

CONVINCED = persuaded in mind; satisfied with evidence

SURE = Certain, unfailing, infallible without doubt

SHAME = That which brings reproach and degrades a person in the estimation of others.

DEFEND = To repel a demand, charge, or accusation; to oppose, to resist.

PROTECT = To cover or shield from danger or injury; to guard; to preserve in safety.

AVENGE = To take satisfaction for an injury by punishing the injuring party; to vindicate!

TIGHTROPE

As I was waking up this morning, I heard out of my spirit again these words:

"Serving the Lord is like walking across a TIGHTROPE."

I did not immediately connect the dots but later thought about the men and women who are funambulists (tightrope walkers). Funambulists, entrust their lives by walking high above the ground with a rope or a thin wire. It takes total CONCENTRATION and FOCUS to walk on a rope or a thin wire high above the ground.

I thought for a moment, if they can entrust their lives with a rope or a thin wire, how much more us ENTRUSTING our lives to our Heavenly Father; the one who created us all? Our Heavenly Father knows everything about everything. He knows how to fix every one of our problems, He knows what it takes for our bodies and minds to be healed and whole, and He knows how to get us out of our messes. He knows how to meet our financial needs and wants. He knows everything about everything. So why not seek and pray to the one who knows everything about everything? Jesus did not leave us without answers or instructions. Jesus told us to *TRUST in the Lord with ALL of our hearts and mind and DO NOT lean or rely on our own insight or understanding. He said to acknowledge Him in all of our ways, and He will DIRECT our paths. (He will show us the shortest way to our deliverance) (Proverbs 3:5 AMPC).*

Jesus said that men ought to *ALWAYS pray and not to turn cowardly (faint, lose heart, and give up) (Luke 18:1 AMPC)*

Jesus also told us to come to him when we labor and are heavy laden. He said that He will give us rest. Let us take His yoke upon us and learn of Him, and we will find rest (relief, ease, refreshment, recreation, and blessed quiet) for our mind, our will, and our emotions. (Matthew 11:28-29 AMPC)

Let us PRACTICE every day OBEYING the words of Jesus and keeping our eyes fixed on Him. In doing so, we will ALL make it across the TIGHTROPE of life with total VICTORY!

Love you ALL to life!

DEFINITIONS:

TIGHTROPE = A rope or wire stretched tightly, high above the ground, on which acrobats perform feats of balancing.

SERVING = Acting in subordination to; yielding obedience to; yielding.

ENTRUST = To put (something) into someone's care or protection.

CONCENTRATE = To bring to a close, union, to bring nearer to each other.

FOCUS = To pay particular attention to.

PRAY = To ask with earnestness or zeal, to entreat, to supplicate.

DIRECT = Moving from one place to another by the shortest way; to point; to show the right road of course.

FAITH IS A REST

Some time ago I encountered a major DEMONIC attack from the enemy. The enemy was closing in on me. I began to feel the pressure of fear, anxiety, worry, and oppression. Note that I said "the enemy" was closing in on me. You see *our fight is not against flesh and blood. Our fight is against the master spirits who are the world's rulers of this present darkness. (Ephesians 6:12).*

The pressure from the enemy began to increase. I then heard these words come out of my spirit:

"A DEEPER TRUST = A DEEPER REST"

Immediately after hearing these words, Jesus began to tell me a story. Jesus said to me, Bernadette, remember when I said to the disciples, "Let us go over to the other side of the lake"? I said, yes Lord! He then said, then a monstrous storm came upon the lake and the waves began to beat upon the disciples and the water filled the boat. I said, yes Lord! Jesus went on to say to me, Bernadette likened the waves that were hitting the disciples to the demonic attacks of fear, anxiety, and oppression that Satan is trying to bring upon and against you. I said, yes Lord! Jesus continued the story by saying, as the water was filling the boat, the disciples came to the hindered part of the boat to wake me up. They began to say "Master we are perishing!" I got up and rebuked the wind and the storm ceased. I again said, yes Lord! (Mark 4:35-39).

After Jesus told me this story, He asked me a very IMPORTANT question. He said to me, "Bernadette why was I able to REST (sleep) in the midst of the storm?"

Before I could even think to answer His question, He gave me the answer. He said, "Bernadette, BECAUSE I TRUSTED MY WORDS." He said, "When you learn to trust my words you will rest also." He said, "A DEEPER TRUST = A DEEPER REST. When I told my disciples that we were going over to the other side of the lake, we were going over. It does not matter what demonic or hellish storms that come your way; no matter what attacks the enemy brings to you, When you TRUST My words, you will come out on the other side, safe, unharmed and with total victory."

I want to encourage you all, that no matter what you are going through; no matter what the enemy is whispering in your ears, saying that you are a failure. Telling you that you will not rise up out of the negative situations and circumstances that have hit you. Even when he attacks you with false accusations to try and ruin your reputation and your name, continue to TRUST His words. The enemy may also be telling you that you will never get well in your body or in your mind. Please DO NOT believe his words. Choose to believe and TRUST God's word (The Holy Bible) and you will see and experience your desired results come to pass.

Satan wants to stop your destiny!!!

Satan is after your TRUST (Faith) in Jehovah God!!!

Do not let him have it.

Love you ALL to life!

DEFINITIONS:

TRUST = Confidence; a reliance or resting of the mind on the integrity, veracity, and justice of another person.

REST = A state free from motion or disturbance; Quiet; a state of reconciliation to God

Remember:

A DEEPER TRUST = A DEEPER REST

GOD'S WORD APPLIED BRINGS POWER

As I was teaching one Sunday morning, I heard out of my spirit:

"GOD'S WORD APPLIED BRINGS POWER."

Jesus left us with these words: Behold I have given you AUTHORITY and POWER to trample upon serpents and scorpions and (physical and mental strength and ability) over all the power that the enemy possesses; and NOTHING shall in any way harm you. (Luke 10:19 AMPC).

Jesus gave us this power, but we must APPLY it to our circumstances in life, in order to see it work on our behalf.

James 1:22-25 states: Be doers of the word, and not hearers only, DECEIVING yourselves. For if anyone is a hearer of the word and not a doer, he is like a man observing his natural face in a mirror; for he observes himself, goes away, and immediately forgets what kind of man he was. But he who looks into the perfect law of liberty and continues in it and is not a forgetful hearer but a doer of the work, this one will be blessed in what he does.

I want to encourage us all to be a doer of God's word. As we APPLY God's word to our lives, we are allowing His POWER to move in our lives and circumstances. If we are not APPLYING God's word to our lives, we open the door to being deceived by others and also deceiving ourselves.

So let us make or continue to make a firm and conscious decision to apply the word of God to every situation and circumstance in our lives. As we do this, we will for sure live a life of peace and freedom (even in the midst of attacks and storms).

Hebrews 4:12 states: For the word of God is living and POWERFUL, and sharper than any two-edged sword, piercing even to the division of soul and spirit, and of joints and marrow, and is a discerner of the thoughts and intents of the heart.

Isaiah 55:11 states: So shall my word be that goes forth from my mouth; it shall not return to me void, But it shall accomplish what I please, And it shall prosper in the thing for which I sent it.

Love you ALL To life!

DEFINITIONS:

AUTHORITY = Legal power; a right to command or act.

POWER = Force; strength, energy, legal authority.

APPLY = To use or employ for a particular purpose

WE ARE CONQUERORS

Amid ALL these things we are more than a CONQUEROR!!!

Yet amid ALL these things we are more than CONQUERORS and gain a surpassing VICTORY through Him (JESUS) who LOVES us. (Rom. 8:37 AMPC)

No, Despite All these things, OVERWHELMING VICTORY is ours through Christ, who LOVES us (Romans 8:37 NLT)

I want to encourage you, that in spite of the ongoing intense pressure that the enemy is bringing upon our nation and upon so many; we have TOTAL VICTORY through Jesus Christ.

Keep on pressing in with prayer and praise, keep on looking away from all of the things that the evil one is doing and look to Jesus!

Jesus is our answer and deliverer.

He has and WILL deliver us. He has already made a way of escape for us.

There is NO temptation or trial that has overtaken us except such as is common to man; but God is FAITHFUL, who will not allow us to be tempted beyond what we are able to bear, but with the temptation and trials, He will also make the way of escape for us, that we may be able to bear it and CONQUER it. (I Corinthians 10:13)

Love you ALL to life!

DEFINITIONS:

AMID = Surrounded by; in the middle of; In an atmosphere or against a background of; In the midst of middle; Among; Mingled with.

CONQUEROR = One who conquers; one who gains a VICTORY; One who subdued and brings into subjection or possession, by force or by influence.

CONQUER = To overcome; To gain the VICTORY

DELIVER = One who releases or rescues; a preserver.

SEEK GOD

The United States of America and other countries around the world are in need of GREAT healing.

We serve a GREAT GOD and a mighty HEALER. (Jehovah God, the God of Abraham, Isaac, and Jacob according to Matthew 22:32 & Acts 3:13)

Our Heavenly Father said that He would heal our land. He left us instructions on how our land can be healed. God gave us a part in seeing to it that the healing takes place. Now the verse that I am giving you is not just a CLICHE, it is more of God's instructions on how to heal The United States of America and the other countries in this world.

II Chronicles 7:14 states: If My people, who are called by My name, will HUMBLE themselves, PRAY, SEEK, crave, and require of necessity My FACE and TURN from their wicked ways, then will I HEAR from heaven, FORGIVE their sin, and HEAL their land.

This is such GREAT NEWS! So I would like to encourage us to turn or continue to turn our eyes and hearts and focus on obeying His instructions! We will NEVER EVER be disappointed when we do so!

Love you ALL to life!

DEFINITIONS:

CALLED = Invited, summoned, appointed, name (We were all invited)

HUMBLE = To reduce arrogance and self-dependence; To abase pride, To make meek and submissive to the divine will; To deprive of chastity.

PRAY = To petition; to ask, as for favor; in worship, to address the supreme being with solemnity and reverence, with adoration, confession of sins, supplication for mercy, and thanksgiving for blessings received.

SEEK = To go in search or quest of; to look for; to inquire for; to ask for; to endeavor to find by any means.

TURN = To change direction to or from any point; to reverse; to change opinions or parties, to repent, to change or shift sides.

FORGIVE = To pardon; to remit as an offense, debt, fine, or penalty; to stop feeling angry or resentful toward (someone) for an offense, flaw, or mistake.

HEAL = To RESTORE to soundness; to return to a sound state; to reconcile; to purify from corruptions.

Please remember this, our Heavenly Father said that if we abide by His instructions, He will HEAR from Heaven and HEAL our land.

Our Heavenly Father is true to his word! I John 5:14-15 states: NOW this is the confidence that we have in Him, that if we ask (petition) anything according to His will (His instructions) He HEARS us, and if we know that HE HEARS us, whatever we ask, we know that we have the petitions that we have asked Him.

CLICHE = a phrase or opinion that is overused and betrays a lack of original thought

IT'S A GREAT DAY

I heard this morning:

"Today is another GREAT day to PRAISE AND WORSHIP THE LORD."

We are all watching this dark evil spirit that is trying to close in on our countries. It seems as if this dark evil spirit is winning. Some may be saying, why is our God standing Idly by and letting it all happen? Well for sure, He is NOT standing idly by.

He who sits in the heavens laughs; the Lord has them in derision (and in supreme contempt, He mocks them). (Psalms 2:4 AMPC)

I was quickly reminded of the story of Jehoshaphat. Three great armies came against Jehoshaphat (the Moabites, the Ammonites, and the Meunites. Fear came upon Jehoshaphat so he began to SEEK the Lord then proclaimed a Fast in all Judah. The people gathered together to seek and ask for help from the Lord. Jehoshaphat stood among the people in the house of the Lord and began to petition God. He also said, "Lord, will you not exercise judgment upon them? For we have no might to stand against this great company that is coming against us, we do not know what to do, but our eyes are upon you". As they looked to the Lord for instructions, The Lord spoke and gave instructions through his prophet Jahaziel. The Lord told them not to be afraid or dismayed at the great armies because the battle is not theirs, but it is His. He instructed the people not to fight in that battle but to take their position and to STAND STILL and see the deliverance of the Lord who was with them. Note! TAKE THEIR POSITION!

Their position was to go out against them by PRAISE and WORSHIP the Lord! Saying give thanks unto the Lord for His mercy and loving-kindness endures forever. When they obeyed the instructions, the Lord set up ambushes against their enemies (Moabites, Ammonites, and Mount Seir). (II Chronicles 20:1-23).

As we, the children of the LIGHT, praise and worship the Lord from our heart we will see this dark evil that has come against us and our countries dissipate before our eyes.

We are VICTORIOUS and we will always win when we follow Our Heavenly Father's instructions.

I want to encourage us ALL to EVERYDAY give PRAISE, WORSHIP, and THANKSGIVING to the Lord!!

For He is TRULY so GOOD!!

Love you ALL To life!

DEFINITIONS:

SEEK = To make search or inquiry; to endeavor

PRAISE = To commend; to applaud; to express approbation of personal worth or actions; to extol in words or songs; to express gratitude of personal favors; to honor; to display the excellence of.

WORSHIP = Honor; to make homage to; to respect.

THANKSGIVING = The act of rendering thanks or expressing gratitude for favors or mercies; a public celebration of divine goodness.

AMBUSHMENT = A private or concealed station, where troops lie in wait to attack their enemy by surprise.

INDEPENDENCE DAY

Why do we celebrate the 4th of July and what does it mean? This day is very significant in American history. It is the day that the United States officially became its own nation. The Declaration of Independence was adopted on July 4th, 1776, and at that time, America was born.

I want to share with you a little history of how it all began!!

Before America was its own country, it was comprised of 13 colonies established by Great Britain. The first colony was settled in Jamestown and Virginia in 1607. European countries, especially Great Britain, continued to colonize America throughout the 17th century and a good portion of the 18th century. By 1775, an estimated 2.5 million settlers lived in the 13 colonies. New Hampshire, Massachusetts, Connecticut, Rhode Island, Delaware, New York, New Jersey, Pennsylvania, Maryland, Virginia, North Carolina and Georgia.

Tensions started brewing when Great Britain began passing legislation that gave it more control within the colonies, especially when it came to taxing the colonists. The Crown was in debt after the French and Indian War, so it started taxing the American colonies to increase revenue. The passage of legislation like the Stamp Act in March 1765, the Townshend Act in June and July of 1767, and the Tea Act of 1773 forced colonists to pay more money to Great Britain even though the colonies didn't have a say in the Crown's Policies. This became known as taxation without representation and quickly became a heated pillar in the foundation of the American Revolution. This led the colonists to seek independence.

This day is the day that we celebrate our FREEDOMS and our GREAT COUNTRY. Let us stand and continue to stand against the tyranny that is trying to be placed upon ALL of us. We have fought too hard with wisdom from God and we have come too far, to allow our FREEDOMS to be taken away from us. We MUST not allow our Constitutional rights to be destroyed and taken away from us.

I want to thank ALL of the soldiers who fought and gave their lives for the freedom of our country!!

I am reminded of this verse in the Holy Bible, which states:

Now the Lord is the Spirit, and where the Spirit of the Lord is, there is liberty
(Emancipation from bondage, freedom.
2 Corinthians 3:17)

I want to encourage us all to keep in our hearts and minds that true FREEDOM is knowing, accepting and walking out what Jesus Christ did at the cross. All other FREEDOMS DERIVES from this FREEDOM. Our Lord and Savior shed His precious blood for us ALL.

He paid the price so that we can all be FREE from any and everything that we need saving and freedom from.

Love you ALL to life!

DEFINITIONS:

FREEDOM = A state of exemption from the power or control of another; liberty; exemption from slavery; servitude or confinement.

COLONY = A company or body of people transplanted from their mother country to a remote province or country to cultivate and inhabit it.

COLONIST = An inhabitant of a colony.

TYRANNY = Cruel and oppressive government or rule; a nation under cruel and oppressive government.

DERIVES = Obtain something from (a specific source); base a concept on a logical extension or modification of another concept.

REVENUE = Income; a states annual income from which public expenses are met.

LEGISLATION = Laws considered; collectively

FOUNDATION = An underlying basis or principle.

REVOLUTION = A forcible overthrow of a government or social order; in favor of a new system.

FREE = Being in liberty; not being under necessity or restraint; not enslaved

SAVING = preserving from evil or destruction; hindering from waste or loss.

EMANCIPATION = The act of setting free from slavery, servitude, subjection or dependence; deliverance from bondage or controlling influence; liberation.

BONDAGE = Slavery or involuntary servitude; captivity; imprisonment; restraint of a person's liberty by compulsion.

WAKE UP

As I was meditating this morning on our Gathering the Troops Bible Study call, I heard these words from my spirit:

"WAKE UP"

I then heard "It is HIGH TIME NOW to wake up out of your sleep". "Let them know to stop sleeping and WAKE UP"

SLEEP-To be careless, inattentive, or unconcerned; Not vigilant.

Romans 13:11-12 (amp) states: Besides this you know what (a critical) hour this is, how it is HIGH TIME NOW for you to WAKE UP out of your sleep (rouse to reality). For SALVATION (final deliverance) is nearer to us now than when we first believed. The NIGHT is far gone, and the DAY is almost here. Let us then drop (fling away) the works and deeds of DARKNESS and put on the FULL ARMOR OF LIGHT. Let us ALL live and conduct ourselves honorably as in the open light of day, not in licentiousness, not in quarreling and jealousy.

I want to encourage us ALL to clothe ourselves with the Lord Jesus Christ, the Messiah. He is absolute LOVE.

For God so loved the world that He gave His only begotten Son, that whoever believes in Him should not perish but have everlasting life.
(St John 3:16)

He loves each and every one of us with His EVERLASTING love. Let's come boldly to Him OK? He will NEVER EVER turn anyone away. He has given ALL who turn to Him, ACCESS TO HIS THRONE, 24 hours a day. Remember this, our Heavenly Father never ever slumbers nor sleep (Psalms 121:3-4)

Love you ALL to life!

DEFINITIONS:

HONORABLY = With tokens of honor or respect; magnanimously; generously; with a noble spirit or purpose.

QUARRELING = Disputing with vehemence or loud angry words; scolding; wrangling; finding fault.

JEALOUSY = Feeling or showing envy of someone or their achievements and advantages.

LICENTIOUSNESS = Excessive indulgence of liberty; contempt of the just restraints of law, morality and decorum.

ARISE

I hear the spirit of the Lord saying:

ARISE from the depression, the heaviness, and prostration in which circumstances have kept you-
ARISE to a new life! Shine (be RADIANT with the GLORY of the Lord), for your LIGHT has come and the glory of the Lord has Risen upon you.
For behold darkness shall cover the earth and dense darkness, but the Lord shall ARISE UPON YOU and His GLORY shall be seen on YOU.
(Isaiah 60:1-2)

If you have accepted Jesus as your Lord and Savior, then you are a child of the most high God; and If you are a child of the most high God, then you are a child of the LIGHT.

Our Heavenly Father promised to give us peace in the midst of the storms of life.

St. John 16:33 (amp) states: I have told you these things, so that in ME you may have perfect PEACE and confidence. In the world you have tribulation and trials and distress and frustration; but be of good cheer (take courage; be confident, certain, undaunted)! For I have overcome the world. (I have deprived it of power to harm you and have conquered it for you).

Let's start walking in that peace, okay?

Don't allow these dark and turbulent times to take you out of the REST of God! Stay connected to the vine (which is Jesus) and execute your God-given authority against ALL of this evil satanic darkness that is upon the earth today. (Luke 10:19).

Remember the true fight is against the darkness, but please ALWAYS remember LIGHT always overcomes DARKNESS! Darkness cannot overpower the Light.

Love you ALL to life!

DEFINITIONS:

ARISE = To ascend, to move from a place of inaction, to be excited, to exert power, to begin to act.

RADIANT = Beaming with brightness

GLORY = Splendor, honor, heavy with everything good.

BE BOLD

Bold and unafraid!!!!

So we take comfort and are encouraged and CONFIDENTLY and BOLDLY say, *The Lord is my Helper; I will NOT be seized with alarm (I WILL NOT FEAR OR DREAD OR BE TERRIFIED) What can man do to me? (Hebrews 13:6 AMP)*

The answer is NOTHING when we put our total trust and confidence in our precious Heavenly Father and In Him alone!!

I woke up this morning with these words coming from my spirit and I would like to encourage you all with these words:

"Be STRONG, BOLD, and COURAGEOUS for the Lord your God is with YOU. He is with YOU wherever YOU go."

Joshua 1:9 states: Have not I commanded you? Be STRONG, VIGOROUS and very COURAGEOUS. Be NOT afraid, neither be dismayed, for your God is with you wherever you go.

I want to also encourage you all to keep before you the light and speak the light, which is God's word.

Remember LIGHT always dispels the DARKNESS.

It will dispel ALL of the enemy's schemes, plots, and plans against you, your family, and this nation.

God is light and in Him is NO darkness at all. (I John 1:5)

So let us all join together and rise up in FAITH and not shrink in fear and please do not GO INTO HIDING!!

Love you ALL to life!

DEFINITIONS:

STRONG = Having the ability to bear or endure; well-fortified, able to sustain attacks; not easily subdued or taken.

VIGOROUS = Full of physical strength or active force; powerful; made by strength, either of body or mind.

COURAGEOUS = Brave; Bold, daring; hardy to encounter difficulties and dangers.

BOLD = Daring; courageous; fearless; brave; requiring courage in the execution; executed with spirit or boldness; confident.

Remember the Lord said for us not to be afraid or dismayed.

AFRAID = Impressed with fear or apprehension, fearful.

Dismayed = Disheartened; deprived of courage.

286

THE COVENANT

The Lord is my LIGHT and my SALVATION whom shall I FEAR or DREAD? **(NO ONE)**

The Lord is the REFUGE and STRONGHOLD of my life of whom shall I be afraid? **(NO ONE)**

When the wicked, (This present darkness and evil) even my enemies and my foes, come upon me to eat up my flesh, they stumbled and fell. Though a host encamps against me my heart shall NOT fear; though war arises against me, (even then) in this will I be confident. One thing have I desired and asked of the Lord, that Will I seek, that I may dwell in His presence ALL the days of my life and behold His beauty and meditate on His LOVE His MERCIES, His KINDNESS, and His FORGIVENESS. For in the day of trouble, He will hide me in His shelter; In the secret place of His tent will he hide me. He will set me (us) high upon a rock. And now shall my head be lifted up above my enemies. I will offer up sacrifices to the Lord and sing praises unto His name. The Lord said to seek His face and His presence as our VITAL need! (Psalms 27)

Let us focus on FORGIVENESS! Our Heavenly Father has forgiven ALL of us by sending His son Jesus to pay the ultimate sacrifice for our past, present and future sins. (St. John 3:16)

Please remember that when we accept Jesus as our Lord and Savior, at that very moment, we entered into a covenant with him. So let's see ourselves as covenant children of a covenant-keeping God! When our precious Heavenly Father gave us Jesus, He gave us EVERYTHING. Let us stop pointing our fingers at each other and blaming each other; Instead, let us get into the word of God and learn of and possess the covenant that was given to us ALL! That means BLACK skin, WHITE skin, BROWN skin, YELLOW skin or BLUE skin.

No HUMAN BEING, No INSTITUTION, or any SYSTEM can hold a person down that knows and understands their covenant (their rights and privileges in Christ)

(Galatians 3:13-15), (Hebrews 9:15-28)

I would like to encourage ALL pastors, teachers, prophets, evangelist and all leaders of faith to teach or continue to teach their congregants or audiences the message of the COVENANT along with the message of LOVE and FORGIVENESS!

I truly believe that when we do this that we will truly see a mighty REVIVAL take place in our world.

Love you ALL to life!

DEFINITIONS:

LIGHT = Illumination of mind; instruction; knowledge

SALVATION = The act of saving; preservation from destruction, danger, or great calamity.

FEAR = A painful emotion or passion excited by an expectation of evil, or the apprehension of impending danger.

REFUGE = To shelter; to protect.

STRONGHOLD = A fastness; a fort; a fortified place; a place of security.

MERCY = Compassion or forgiveness shown toward someone whom it is within one's power to punish or harm.

KINDNESS = The quality of being friendly, generous, and considerate.

FORGIVENESS = The act of forgiving; the pardon of an offender, by which he is considered and treated as not guilty.

BE ENCOURAGED

God is our REFUGE and STRENGTH, a very PRESENT and well-proved help in TROUBLE!!! Therefore, we WILL NOT FEAR, though the earth should change and though the mountains be shaken into the midst of the seas. Psalms 46:1-2 (AMP)

Be encouraged and rest, trust and lean on the truth of these words!! They will totally carry you through these challenging times NOW and throughout your ENTIRE life.

Love you ALL to life!

DEFINITIONS:

REFUGE = Shelter or protection from danger or distress.

STRENGTH = Power of resisting attacks; Security

PRESENT= Existing or occurring now (a right now help)

TROUBLE = Unrest, uproar, disorder, worry, anxiety, distress, stress, concern, conflict, harassment, and difficulty or problems.

LOVE WINS

A word that came to me in the middle of the night:

In making many books there is no end and much study is weariness of the flesh. Let us hear the conclusion of the whole matter, fear God (revere & worship Him) and keep His COMMANDMENTS; for this is the whole duty of man (the full, original purpose of His creation, the object of God's providence, the root of character, the foundation of ALL inharmonious circumstances and conditions under the sun). (Ecclesiastes 12:12-14)

God's COMMANDMENT is that we walk in LOVE.

St. John 14:12 states: This is my commandment, that you love one another just as I have loved you.

This love is both understanding how much the Father loves us and how we are to love each other.

SO, WHAT IS LOVE?

I Corinthians 13:4-8 (AMP) gives us a good description of what God's kind of love is. It states: Love endures long and is patient and kind; love never is envious nor boils over with jealousy, is not boastful or vainglorious, does not display itself haughtily, it is not conceited (arrogant and inflated with pride), it is not rude (unmannerly) and does not act unbecomingly. Love (God's love in us) does not insist on it's own rights or it's own way, for it is not SELF SEEKING; it is not touchy or fretful or resentful; It takes NO ACCOUNT of the evil done to it (it pays NO attention to a suffered wrong). It does NOT rejoice at injustice and unrighteousness but REJOICES when right and truth prevails. Love bears up under anything and everything that comes, and is EVER ready to BELIEVE the BEST of EVERY PERSON. It's hope is fade-less under ALL circumstances, and it endures everything (WITHOUT WEAKENING)

LOVE NEVER FAILS ....

Everything else will fail, but LOVE will NEVER fail **BECAUSE GOD IS LOVE.**

I JOHN 4:7: Beloved, let us love one another, for love is of God; and everyone who loves is born of God and knows God.

Understanding and having a revelation of how much our Heavenly Father loves us is TOTALLY VITAL to us living a FEARLESS life that is free from depression, anxiety and torment.

The Bible says, "There is NO fear in LOVE, but perfect love drives away (casts out) ALL fear" (I John 4:8)

Our Heavenly Father wants us to have FAITH in His LOVE for us. He loves us with an everlasting love (Jeremiah 31:3)

John 3:16 (AMP): He loved mankind so much that He Sent His only begotten son, Jesus, to the cross to pay the penalty for our sins (past, present, and future).

He paid for all our diseases and freedom from all forms of lack.

Our part is to make Jesus Lord over our lives by confessing with our mouths and believing in our hearts that God raised Jesus from the dead and then we shall be saved (Romans 10:9-10).

Our day-to-day walk should reflect this confession.

Christ was made manifest (visible) for the purpose of undoing (destroying, loosening, and dissolving the works of the evil one (the devil). (I John 3:8 AMP)

I want to urge every person to receive (accept) the LOVE that our Heavenly Father has for us and also by loving each other the way He commanded us to in I Corinthians 13:4-8.

Jesus said those who really love Him, will obey His word and that He will manifest (make known) Himself to them. (St. John 14:21 & 23)

Let us ALL remember that we were created, destined, and appointed to live for the praise of God's Glory, not our Glory!! (Ephesians 1:12)

This is TRUE PEACE and the FOUNDATION of ALL our happiness!

Love you ALL to life!

DEFINITIONS:

VITAL = Very necessary; highly important; essential.

FEARLESS = Freedom from fear; courage; boldness; intrepidity.

SELF-SEEKING = Having concern for one's own welfare and interests before those of others; self-serving.

FAITH = Belief; the assent of the mind to the truth of what is declared by another, resting on his authority and veracity, without other evidence.

PEACE = A state of quiet or tranquility; freedom from disturbance or agitation.

FOUNDATION = The basis of an edifice; the basis or groundwork, of anything; that on which anything stands.

ANXIETY = Concern or solicitude respecting some event, future or uncertain, which disturbs the mind, and keeps it in a state of painful uneasiness.

TORMENT = To put to extreme pain or anguish; to inflict excruciating pain and misery, either of body or mind.

DARKNESS AND GROSS DARKNESS

I was awakened early one morning, and I heard myself saying:

"Lord, what's coming on the face of the earth"?

The response was "Darkness and Gross Darkness", then I heard "BUT I will SAVE my people"; "I will RESCUE my people".

He went on to say, "Stay in the LIGHT as He, JESUS, is the light"!

STAY IN JESUS!

The word SAVE means to preserve from injury, destruction, or evil of any kind; to rescue from danger; to preserve from final & everlasting destruction; to rescue from eternal death!

The word RESCUE means to be FREE from any confinement, violence, danger or evil; to remove or withdraw from a state of EXPOSURE to evil; taking away lawful distress!

Isaiah 60:1-3 (AMP) states: ARISE (from the depression and prostration in which circumstances have kept you-RISE to a NEW life! Shine (be radiant with the GLORY of the Lord), for YOUR LIGHT has come, and the GLORY of the Lord has risen upon you! For behold, darkness shall cover the earth, and dense darkness (all) peoples, BUT the Lord shall RISE upon YOU and His GLORY shall be seen upon YOU!!

Nations shall come to YOUR light, and kings to the BRIGHTNESS of your RISING!

St. John 1:4-5 states: In HIM (JESUS) was LIFE, and the LIFE was the LIGHT of men. And the LIGHT shines on in the darkness, for the darkness has NEVER overpowered it!

God is ABSOLUTELY LIGHT and there is ABSOLUTELY NO darkness in Him!!! (I John 1:5)

Remember precious children of our Heavenly Father, you are the children of the LIGHT!! Stand strong in the LIGHT and you will see total victory in your life.

Love you ALL to life!

VACCINATE YOURSELF WITH THE WORD OF GOD

~ Psalm 91 (NKJV) ~

He who dwells in the secret place of the Most High

Shall abide under the shadow of the Almighty.

I will say of the Lord, "He is my refuge and my fortress;

My God, in Him I will trust."

Surely He shall deliver you from the snare of the fowler

And from the perilous pestilence.

He shall cover you with His feathers,

And under His wings you shall take refuge;

His truth shall be your shield and buckler.

You shall not be afraid of the terror by night,

Nor of the arrow that flies by day,

Nor of the pestilence that walks in darkness,

Nor of the destruction that lays waste at noonday.

A thousand may fall at your side,

And ten thousand at your right hand;

But it shall not come near you.

Only with your eyes shall you look,

And see the reward of the wicked.

Because you have made the Lord, who is my refuge,

Even the Most High, your dwelling place,

No evil shall befall you,

Nor shall any plague come near your dwelling;

For He shall give His angels charge over you,

To keep you in all your ways.

In their hands they shall bear you up,

Lest you dash your foot against a stone.

You shall tread upon the lion and the cobra,

The young lion and the serpent you shall trample underfoot.

"Because he has set his love upon Me, therefore I will deliver him;

I will set him on high because he has known My name.

He shall call upon Me, and I will answer him;

I will be with him in trouble;

I will deliver him and honor him.

With long life I will satisfy him,

And show him My salvation."

Let us ALL vaccinate ourselves and our household with Psalms 91 EVERYDAY!!

You will be kept safe from ALL hidden DANGER, ALL DEADLY DISEASES, and NO DISASTER will strike you and NO VIOLENCE will come nigh your home!! (Psalms 91:10 GNB)

Love you ALL to life!

UNIFY AROUND THE TRUTH

The spirit of confusion, division, backbiting, accusation, deception, gossip, name-calling, slandering and dishonesty

<u>MUST STOP!!!</u>

You may be asking how do we stop it?

We can stop it by replacing it with the TRUTH! What is the truth? God's word is the truth!! (St. John 17:17).

If we will all take the time to read and pray the word of God and focus on our Judeo Christian Values (the values that our United States Constitution was built upon), and practice and live by them, all the confusion, division, backbiting, accusations, deception, name calling, slandering and dishonesty will begin to cease!

The goal of the enemy is to keep everyone in a state of confusion and unrest in our minds so that he can ultimately destroy us all.

I want to encourage you not to join his (the devil) team. If you have joined his team, quickly remove yourself from it before destruction comes.

The thief (the enemy) comes to steal, kill and destroy. (St. John 10:10).

I want to also urge us to put our PETTY differences aside.

Let's focus on what UNITES us and RISE above what divides us.

We must unify around the truth.

If you have a concern or an issue with an individual, please go directly to them and INQUIRE of them. This will help to stop negative rumors etc.

You will be totally amazed and thankful at the PEACE that you will begin to experience when you practice and live by the truth.

LOVE TRULY WINS!!!

Love you ALL to life!

DEFINITIONS:

CONFUSION = lack of understanding; uncertainty; In a general sense, a mixture of several things promiscuously.

DIVISION = The act of dividing or separating into parts, any entire body; disagreement between two or more groups, typically producing tension or hostility.

BACKBITING = The act of slandering the absent; secret calumny; malicious talk about someone who is not present.

ACCUSATION = The act of accusing of any wrong or injustice; the action or process of accusing someone.

DECEPTION = The act of deceiving or misleading; The state of being deceived or misled.

GOSSIP = Casual or unconstrained conversation or reports about other people, typically involving details that are not confirmed as being true;

To run about and tattle; to tell idle tales.

NAME CALLING = A form of argument in which insulting or demeaning labels are directed at an individual or group.

SLANDER = To make false and damaging statements about someone.

DISHONESTY = Deceitful shown in someone's character or behavior; want of probity, or integrity in principle; faithlessness; a disposition to cheat or defraud, or to deceive and betray.

TRUTH = Conformity to fact or reality; God's Word.

FOCUS = A central point; point of concentration; pay particular attention to.

PRACTICE = To perform certain acts frequently or customarily; perform (an activity) or exercise (a skill) repeatedly or regularly in order to improve or maintain one's proficiency.

CEASE = To stop moving, acting, or speaking; to leave off; bring or come to an end.

GOAL = The end or final purpose; the object of a person's ambition or effort; an aim or desired result.

UNREST = A state of dissatisfaction, disturbance, and agitation in a group of people, typically involving public demonstrations or disorder; Unquietness; uneasiness.

ULTIMATELY = Finally; at last; at the end or last consequence. Afflictions often tend to correct immoral habits; finally; in the end.

DESTROY = To demolish; to pull down; to separate the parts of an edifice, the union of which is necessary to constitute the thing; to ruin; to bring to naught.

ENCOURAGE = To give courage to; to give or increase the confidence of success; to inspire with courage, spirit, or strength of mind; to embolden; to animate; to incite; to inspirit.

JOIN = To set or bring one thing in contiguity with another; To unite.

DESTRUCTION = The act of destroying; demolition; pulling down; subversion; ruin, by whatever means.

THIEF = One who secretly, unlawfully, and feloniously takes the goods or personal property of another.

STEAL = To take and carry away feloniously, as the personal goods of another; take (another person's property) without permission or legal right and without intending to return it.

KILL = To deprive of life, animal or vegetable, in any manner or by any means; put an end to or cause the failure or defeat of (something).

URGE = Try earnestly or persistently to persuade (someone) to do something.

PETTY = Of little importance; trivial. Small; little; trifling; inconsiderable; as a petty trespass.

UNITE = To join in an act; to concur; to come or bring together for a common purpose or action.

RISE = To move or pass upward in any manner; to ascend; move from a lower position to a higher one; come or go up.

DIVIDE = To cause to be separate; to keep apart.

to part or separate an entire thing.

INQUIRE = To ask a question; to seek for truth or information by asking questions.

NEGATIVE = Consisting of in or characterized by the absence rather than the presence of distinguishing features; of a person, attitude, or situation) not desirable or optimistic.

RUMOR = Flying or popular report; a current story passing from one person to another, without any known authority for the truth of it; a currently circulating story or report of uncertain or doubtful truth.

AMAZE = surprise (someone) greatly; fill with astonishment; to fill with wonder: astound.

PEACE = A state of quiet or tranquility; freedom from disturbance or agitation.

EXPERIENCE = Observation of a fact or of the same facts or events happening under like circumstances; Knowledge derived from trials, use, practice, or from a series of observations.

PRACTICE = To do or perform frequently, customarily, or habitually; to perform by a succession of acts.

LOVE = God is love; in a general sense to be pleased with; to regard with affection, on account of some qualities which excite pleasing sensations or desire of gratification.

WIN = To gain victory; To gain ground; be successful or victorious in (a contest or conflict).

SO MUCH NOISE

As I was waking, I heard these words:

Noise, Noise, and More Noise!

Talk, Talk, and More Talk!

Accusations, Accusations, and more Accusations!

Whisper, Whisper, and more Whisper!

Slander, Slander and more Slander!

This ought not to be!!

All of this is coming to take one's FOCUS off the truth or from seeing the truth! It is sent to try and stop one from fulfilling their God given destiny in this life.

It is sent to try and stop one from discovering their purpose and calling in this life.

It is sent to paralyze and cripple one's mind.

It is sent to bring fear and torment.

It is also sent to stop the accusers, whisperers, slanderers, and noisemakers from walking out of their destiny and purpose and preventing them from living in true peace. The Bible says that there is NO peace for the wicked. (Isaiah 48:22)

These are all ONLY mere distractions. Do NOT allow any of this to move or take you away from your purpose or from finding out your purpose and calling.

Stay tunnel-vision and laser-focused on the truth.

Hebrews tells us to look away [from all that will distract] to Jesus, Who is the Leader and the Source of our faith [giving the first incentive for our belief] and is also its Finisher [bringing it to maturity and perfection]. (Hebrews 12:2 AMP)

I have discovered and come to the realization that our Heavenly Father knows everything about everything.

So why not inquire and look to Him for our answers?

He will NEVER EVER lead us astray or lead us down the wrong path. He will always lead us to the truth and give us the necessary strategies and plans. He will lead and guide us to our purpose and our calling in this life.

As long as there is breath within us, it is NEVER too late to fulfill and walk out our purpose and fulfill our destiny.

I want to encourage you NEVER EVER to allow ANYTHING, ANY CIRCUMSTANCES, ANY FAILURES, ANY ACCUSATIONS, ANY FALSE ACCUSATIONS, or ANY HUMAN BEING to paralyze you and to take you from focusing on and fulling your destiny and purpose in this life.

I also want to encourage us all not to ever be COMPLICIT with evil or wrongdoings. Keep laser-focused on the truth and on getting the TRUTH OUT. The truth will expose and eradicate evil and wrongdoings.

On the other hand, let's try and find the good in people and PROMOTE the good.

You will discover that even through all of the turbulence that is going on in our world today, you can live with so much <u>PEACE</u>, <u>JOY</u>, <u>CONFIDENCE</u>, and <u>CONTENTMENT</u>.

Love you ALL to life!

DEFINITIONS:

NOISE = To spread by rumor or report; Frequent talk; much public conversation.

TALK = Report; rumor; To converse familiarly; to speak, as in familiar discourse, when two or more persons interchange thoughts.

ACCUSATION = The act of charging with a crime or offense; the act of accusing of any wrong or injustice;

a charge or claim that someone has done something illegal or wrong.

ACCUSER = One who accuses or blames; an officer who prefers an accusation against another for some offense, in the name of the government, before a tribunal that has cognizance of the offense;

a person who claims that someone has committed an offense or done something wrong.

WHISPER = To plot secretly; to devise mischief; to speak with suspicion or timorous caution.

WHISPERER = A backbiter; one who slanders secretly. A tattler; one who tells secrets; a conveyer of intelligence secretly.

SLANDER = A false tale or report maliciously uttered, and tending to injure the reputation of another by lessening him in the esteem of his fellow citizens, by exposing him to impeachment and punishment, or by impairing his means of living; defamation To defame; to injure by maliciously uttering a false report respecting one; to tarnish or impair the reputation of one by false tales, maliciously told or propagated.

FOCUS = A central point; point of concentration; pay particular attention to.

PATH = Course of life; the course or direction in which a person or thing is moving.

TRUTH = God's Word; Conformity to fact or reality; exact accordance with that which is, or has been, or shall be.

DESTINY = State or condition appointed or predetermined; ultimate fate; as, men are solicitous to know their future destiny, which is however happily concealed from them; future that someone or something will have.

PURPOSE = To intend; to design; to resolve; to determine on some end or object to be accomplished. The reason for which something is done or created or for which something exists.

CALLING = Vocation; profession; trade; usual occupation, or employment. strong urge toward a particular way of life or career; a vocation.

FULFILLING = Accomplishing; performing; completing.

DISCOVERING = Uncovering; disclosing to view; laying open; revealing; making known; espying; finding out; detecting.

PARALYZE = Render (someone) unable to think or act normally, especially through panic or fear. Cause (a person or part of the body) to become partly or wholly incapable of movement.

CRIPPLE = To disable; to deprive of the power of exertion; cause severe and disabling damage to; deprive of the ability to function normally.

FEAR = A painful emotion or passion excited by an expectation of evil, or the apprehension of impending danger; False Evidence Appearing Real.

TORMENT = To put to extreme pain or anguish; to inflict excruciating pain and misery, either of body or mind; severe physical or mental suffering.

PEACE = A state of quiet or tranquility; freedom from disturbance or agitation; applicable to society, to individuals, or to the temper of the mind; Freedom from private quarrels, suits, or disturbance.

Freedom from agitation or disturbance by the passions, as from fear, terror, anger, anxiety or the like; quietness of mind; tranquility; calmness; quiet of conscience.

WICKED = Evil in principle or practice; deviating from the divine law; addicted to vice; sinful; immoral. This is a word of comprehensive signification, extending to everything that is contrary to the moral law, and both to persons and actions. persons who live in sin; transgressors of the divine law; all who are unreconciled to God, unsanctified or impenitent. Intended to or capable of harming someone or something.

DISTRACTION = Confusion from a multiplicity of objects crowding on the mind and calling the attention in different ways; perturbation of mind; perplexity. The act of distracting; a drawing apart; separation. Confusion of affairs; tumult; disorder.

TUNNEL VISION = The tendency to focus exclusively on a single or limited goal or point of view.

LASER FOCUS = The mental ability to give 100 percent of your attention to the task you've prioritized in the present moment.

FAITH = Belief; the assent of the mind to the truth of what is declared by another, resting on his authority and veracity, without other evidence; the judgment that what another states or testifies is the truth. The assent of the mind or understanding of the truth of what God has revealed.

DISCOVER = To uncover; to remove a covering. To lay open to the view; to disclose; to show; to make visible; to expose to view something before unseen or concealed. To reveal; to make known.

REALIZE = To become fully aware of (something) as a fact; understand clearly.

REALIZATION = The act of realizing or making real; The act of believing or considering as real.

INQUIRE = To ask a question; to seek truth or information by asking questions.

ASTRAY = Away from the correct path or direction. Out of the right way or proper place, both in a literal and figurative sense. In morals and religion, it signifies wandering from the path of rectitude, from duty and happiness.

STRATEGIES = A plan of action or policy designed to achieve a major or overall aim.

PLANS = A detailed proposal for doing or achieving something.

A scheme devised; a project; the form of something to be done existing in the mind, with the several parts adjusted in idea, expressed in words or committed to writing.

LEAD = To guide or conduct by showing the way; to direct.

To guide by the hand; as, to lead a child.

GUIDE = A person who leads or directs another in his way or course.

One who directs another in his conduct or course of life.

COMPLICIT = Involved with others in an illegal activity or wrongdoing; helping to commit a crime or do wrong in some way.

EXPOSE = To lay open; to set to public view; to disclose; to uncover or draw from concealment. reveal the true, objectionable nature of (someone or something).

ERADICATE = To destroy thoroughly; to extirpate. destroy completely; put an end to it. To pull up the roots or by the roots. Hence, to destroy anything that grows; to extirpate; to destroy the roots, so that the plant will not be reproduced; as to eradicate weeds.

PROMOTE = To forward; to advance; to contribute to the growth, enlargement, or excellence of anything valuable. further the progress of (something, especially a cause, venture, or aim); support or actively encourage. Advance or raise (someone) to a higher position or rank

TURBULENCE = A disturbed state; tumult; confusion; as the turbulence of the times; turbulence in political affairs. Disposition to resist authority, insubordination. Characterized by conflict, disorder, or confusion; not controlled or calm.

JOY = To gladden; to exhilarate. To enjoy; to have or possess with pleasure, or to have pleasure in the possession of; a feeling of great pleasure and happiness.

CONFIDENCE = A trusting, or reliance; an assurance of mind or firm belief in the integrity, stability, or veracity of another, or in the truth and reality of a fact. That in which trust is placed; ground of trust; he or that which supports.

CONTENTMENT = Content; a resting or satisfaction of mind without disquiet; acquiescence; Gratification. A state of happiness and satisfaction

YOUR PLAN

I heard these words while I was praying early this morning:

"Your plan Your plan Your plan! Lord it's your plan that I want"!

It is Your plan that will be blessed!

It is Your plan that will bring true peace!

It is Your plan that will bring true prosperity!

ONLY Your plan!!!

Our Heavenly Father has an amazing plan for each and every one of us. It is so important that we follow His plan for our lives.

There is total safety, security, peace, joy and excitement in following His plan. Even through the attacks that come your way, as you follow him, there will be a deep settled peace within you.

Riches may come in one following their own plans, but it is the Lord's plan that will prosper one with NO sorrow attached to it.

I want to encourage you all to seek after and follow the Lord's plan for your life. You will be amazingly surprised and blessed!!

In Jeremiah 29:11 it states: For I know the thoughts and plans that I have for you, thoughts and plans for welfare and peace and NOT for evil, to give you hope in your final outcome.

In Proverbs 10:22 The blessing of the Lord—it makes [truly] rich, and He adds NO sorrow with it [neither does toiling increase it]".

Love you ALL to life!

DEFINITIONS:

STAND = To succeed; to maintain one's ground; not to fail; to continue unchanged or valid; not to fail or become void; to be fixed or steady; not to vacillate; to have a direction; to be permanent; to endure.

TEST = That with which anything is compared for proof of its genuineness; a standard; take measures to check the quality, performance, or reliability of (something), especially before

putting it into widespread use or practice. A procedure intended to establish the quality, performance, or reliability of something, especially before it is taken into widespread use.

BLESSED = Happy; prosperous in worldly affairs; enjoying spiritual happiness and the favor of God; enjoying heavenly felicity.

THOUGHTS = Properly, that which the mind thinks. Thought is either the act or operation of the mind, when attending to a particular subject or thing, or it is the idea consequent on that operation. An idea or opinion produced by thinking or occurring suddenly in the mind.

PLAN = A detailed proposal for doing or achieving something; an intention or decision about what one is going to do; decide on and arrange in advance; design or make a plan of. (Something to be made or built).

WELFARE = Exemption from misfortune, sickness, calamity or evil; the enjoyment of health and the common blessings of life; prosperity; happiness. Exemption from any unusual evil or calamity; the enjoyment of peace and prosperity, or the ordinary blessings of society and

civil government.

PEACE = Freedom from agitation or disturbance by the passions, as from fear, terror, anger, anxiety or the like; quietness of mind; tranquility; calmness; quiet of conscience. Freedom from internal commotion or civil war. Harmony; concord; a state of reconciliation

between parties at variance. A state or period in which there is no war, or a war has ended.

EVIL = Not well; not with justice or propriety; unsuitably. Unfortunate; unhappy; producing sorrow, distress, injury or calamity; as evil tidings; evil arrows; evil days. Having bad qualities of a moral kind; wicked; corrupt; perverse; wrong; as evil thoughts; evil deeds; evil speaking; an evil generation.

HOPE = Confidence in a future event; the highest degree of well-founded expectation of good as a hope founded on God's gracious promises. That which gives hope; he or that which furnishes ground of expectation or promises desired good. The hope of Israel is the Messiah. To place confidence in; to trust in with confident expectation of good.

FINAL = Pertaining to the end or conclusion; last; ultimate.

OUTCOME = The way a thing turns out; a consequence; to place confidence in; to trust in with confident expectation of good.

FINAL OUTCOME = A final product or end result.

FOLLOWING = Coming or going after or behind; pursuing; attending; imitating; succeeding in time; resulting from, as an effect or an inference; adhering to; obeying, observing; using, practicing; proceeding in the same course.

PROSPERITY = Advance or gain in anything good or desirable; successful progress in any business or enterprise; success; attainment of the object desired; as the prosperity of arts; agricultural or commercial prosperity; national prosperity. Our disposition to abuse the blessings of providence renders; the state of being Prosperous.

PROSPEROUS = Successful in material terms.

SAFETY = Freedom from danger or hazard; as the safety of an electrical experiment; the safety of a voyage; Exemption from hurt, injury or loss.

SECURITY = Protection; effectual defense or safety from danger of any kind.

JOY = To enjoy; to have or possess with pleasure, or to have pleasure in the possession of; To gladden; to exhilarate; a feeling of great pleasure and happiness.

EXCITEMENT = The act of exciting; stimulation; the state of being roused into action, or of having increased action; a feeling of great enthusiasm and eagerness.

ATTACK = To fall upon, with unfriendly words or writing; to begin a controversy with; to attempt to overthrow or bring into disrepute, by satire, calumny or criticism; as, to attack a man or his opinions in a pamphlet.

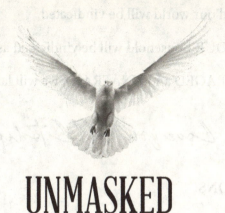

UNMASKED

While I was getting ready the other morning, I heard these words:

"UNMASKED" "UNMASKING" "THINGS ARE BEING UNMASKED"

Right after I heard these words, I then heard:

"The TRUTH is being revealed and the evil, ALL OF THE EVIL, is being exposed."

Things may not have happened in our time frame but be assured evil is being uncovered. It is coming to the surface for all to see.

ECCLESIASTES 8:11-13 states: Because sentence against an evil work is not executed speedily, therefore the heart of the sons of men is fully set in them to do evil.

So, do not be discouraged when you see it and hear it surfacing. It will come up and It will be eradicated and destroyed!!

America and our world will be vindicated.

YOU and YOUR household will be vindicated as well.

Be ENCOURAGED and UNAFRAID, we will land safely!!!

Love you ALL to life!

DEFINITIONS:

UNMASKED = Stripped of a mask or disguise; Open; exposed to view

UNMASKING = to reveal the true nature of: expose. : to remove a mask from.

EVIL = Having bad qualities of a moral kind; wicked; corrupt; perverse; wrong; Having bad qualities of a natural kind; mischievous; having qualities which tend to injure, or to produce mischief. Unfortunate; unhappy; producing sorrow, distress, injury or calamity.

TRUTH = God's Word; The Holy Bible; Conformity to fact or reality; exact accordance with that which is, or has been, or shall be. The truth of history constitutes its whole value. We rely on the truth of the scriptural prophecies.

EXPOSED = Laid open; laid bare; uncovered; unprotected; made liable to attack; offered for sale; disclosed; made public; offered to view. To lay open; to set to public view; to disclose; to uncover or draw from concealment.

TIME FRAME = a period of time, especially a specified period in which something occurs or is planned to take place.

ASSURE = To make certain; to give confidence by a promise, declaration, or other evidence; To confirm; to make certain or secure.

UNCOVERED = Divested of a covering or clothing; laid open to view; made bare; not covered.

SURFACE = the outside part or uppermost layer of something (often used when describing its texture, form, or extent). Relating to or occurring on the upper or outer part of something.

SURFACING = Rise or come up to the surface of the water or the ground; provide (something, especially a road) with a particular upper or outer layer.

EXECUTED = Done; performed; accomplished; carried into effect; put to death. carry out or put into effect (a plan, order, or course of action.

DISCHARGED = Unloaded; let off; shot; thrown out; dismissed from service; paid; released; acquitted; freed from debt or penalty; liberated; performed; executed.

ERADICATED = Plucked up by the roots; extirpated; destroyed.

DESTROYED = Demolished; pulled down; ruined; annihilated; devoured; swept away.

VINDICATED = Defended; supported; maintained; proved to be just or true. Clear (someone) of blame or suspicion.

HOUSEHOLD = Those who dwell under the same roof and compose a family; those who belong to a family.

ENCOURAGE = To give courage to; to give or increase confidence of success; to inspire with courage, spirit, or strength of mind; to embolden; to animate; to incite; to inspirit.

UNAFRAID = feeling no fear or anxiety.

HONOR

Let's honor all of those who died in active military service.

These brave, selfless and courageous men and women put their lives on the line so that we could be FREE and so that we could remain FREE.

Let's not allow our freedoms to be stripped, stolen or taken from us.

Let us all UNITE and RALLY around the truth. Let us lock arms together and move forward.

Let's not shrink back in fear but let us rise up in faith.

It is vital that we educate ourselves, our children and our communities regarding the truth about history.

If we do not educate ourselves regarding true history etc., we could be deceived and accept the lies that have been and are still being told to us.

We must know and value our U.S. Constitution. We also must know, understand and value the price that our soldiers paid and are still paying to keep us protected.

As I began to think about these brave soldiers and the price that they have paid, I could not help but think about our Lord and Savior Jesus Christ.

Our Lord and Savior Jesus Christ paid the ultimate price. He gave His life so that ALL men could have eternal life.

He died on the cross and was risen on the third day so that we could be totally FREE (Luke 24:6-7)

- Free from anxiety.
- Free from worry.
- Free from fear.
- Free from torment.
- Free from oppression.
- Free from depression.
- Free from all addictions.

Free from all the yokes and bondages of the evil enemy.

For whom the son sets free is free indeed. (John 8:36)

I want to encourage us all to walk and continue to walk and live in this freedom!

Love you ALL to life!

DEFINITIONS:

HONOR = The esteem due or paid to worth; high estimation; high respect; great esteem.

BRAVE = To defy; to challenge; to encounter with courage and fortitude, or without being moved; to set at defiance.

SELFLESS = Concerned more with the needs and wishes of others than with one's own; unselfish.

COURAGEOUS = Brave; bold; daring; intrepid; hardy to encounter difficulties and dangers; adventurous.

FREE = To cover or shield from danger or injury; to defend; to guard; to preserve in safety. In government, not enslaved; not in a state of vassalage or dependence; subject only to fixed laws, made by consent, and to a regular administration of such laws; not subject to the arbitrary will of a sovereign or lord; as a free state, nation or people.

FREEDOM = A state of exemption from the power or control of another; liberty; exemption from slavery, servitude or confinement.

STRIPPED = Pulled or torn off; peeled; skinned; deprived; divested; made naked; impoverished; husked, as maiz.

STOLEN = To steal.

STEAL = Take (another person's property) without permission or legal right and without intending to return it.

TAKEN = Received; caught; apprehended; captivated; remove (someone or something) from a particular place.

UNITE = Come or bring together for a common purpose or action. To join in an act; to concur; to act in concert.

RALLY = To reunite; to collect and reduce to order troops dispersed or thrown into confusion; To come back to order.

TRUTH = God's word; Conformity to fact or reality; exact accordance with that which is, or has been, or shall be.

VITAL = Very necessary; highly important; essential.

EDUCATE = To bring up, as a child; to instruct; to inform and enlighten the understanding; to instill into the mind principles of arts, science, morals, religion and behavior. To educate children well is one of the most important duties of parents and guardians. Give (someone) training in or information on a particular field.

HISTORY = An account of facts, particularly of facts respecting nations or states; a narration of events in the order in which they happened.

The study of past events, particularly in human affairs.

DECEIVE = To mislead the mind; to cause to err; to cause to believe what is false or disbelieve what is true; to impose on; to delude.

CONSTITUTION = The established form of government in a state, kingdom or country; a system of fundamental rules, principles and ordinances for the government of a state or nation. In free states, the constitution is paramount to the statutes or laws enacted by the legislature, limiting and controlling its power; and in the United States, the legislature is created, and its powers designated, by the constitution.

PROTECT = To cover or shield from danger or injury; to defend; to guard; to preserve in safety.

VALUE = To rate at a high price; to have in high esteem. The regard that something is held to deserve, the importance, worth, or usefulness of something.

ULTIMATE = Final; being that to which all the rest is directed, as to the main object.

ANXIETY = Concern or solicitude respecting some event, future or uncertain, which disturbs the mind, and keeps it in a state of painful uneasiness.

FEAR = A painful emotion or passion excited by an expectation of evil, or the apprehension of impending danger.

WORRY = To tease; to trouble; to harass with importunity, or with care and anxiety.

TORMENT = To put to extreme pain or anguish; to inflict excruciating pain and misery, either of body or mind. To tease; to vex; to harass.

OPPRESSION = The act of oppressing; the imposition of unreasonable burdens, either in taxes or services; cruelty; severity. A sense of heaviness or weight in the breast.

DEPRESSION = The act of pressing down; or the state of being pressed down; a low state. A sinking of the spirits; dejection; a state of sadness.

ADDICTION = The act of devoting or giving up in practice; the state of being devoted.

BONDAGE = Slavery or involuntary servitude; captivity; imprisonment; restraint of a Person's liberty by compulsion.

ENEMY = A foe; an adversary. A private enemy is one who hates another and wishes him injury or attempts to do him injury to gratify his own malice or ill will.

INDEED = In reality; in truth; in fact. Used to introduce a further and stronger or more surprising point.

VINDICATION

Jesus said, "PEACE I leave with You; My own peace I NOW give and bequeath to you. Not as the world gives do I give to you. Do NOT let your hearts be troubled, neither let it be afraid. Stop allowing yourselves to be agitated and disturbed; and do not permit yourselves to be fearful and intimidated and cowardly and unsettled..." (St. John 14:27)

He went on to say, "I have told you these things, so that in Me you may have perfect peace and confidence. In the world you will have tribulation and trials and distress and frustration;

but be of good cheer (take courage; be confident, certain, undaunted) For I have OVERCOME the world. I HAVE DEPRIVED IT OF POWER TO HARM YOU AND HAVE

CONQUERED IT FOR YOU". (St. John 16:33).

I want to encourage you all, NOT to fear or be afraid of what you are seeing, hearing, feeling or even experiencing in life today.

Our Heavenly Father is with us.

It may seem to some, that He is standing idly by with His arms crossed. NO He is not.

Vindication will come and you will SEE and EXPERIENCE it!

Love you ALL to life!

DEFINITIONS:

TROUBLE = To agitate; to disturb; to put into confused motion; To disturb; to perplex; To afflict; to grieve; To distress; cause distress or anxiety to; Public unrest or disorder.

AFRAID = Impressed with fear or apprehension; fearful; Worried that something undesirable will occur or be done; unwilling or reluctant to do something for fear of the consequences; Feeling fear or anxiety; frightened.

AGITATED = Tossed from side to side; shaken; moved violently and irregularly; disturbed; Feeling or appearing troubled or nervous.

DISTURB = Confusion; disorder; Stirred; moved; excited; discomposed; disquieted; agitated; uneasy; interfere with the normal arrangement or functioning of; Interrupt the sleep, relaxation, or privacy of. cause to feel anxious.

FEARFUL = Affected by fear; feeling pain in expectation of evil; Timid; timorous; wanting courage. Feeling afraid; showing fear or anxiety.

INTIMIDATED = To make fearful; to inspire with fear; to dishearten; to bash. Now guilt once harbored in the conscious breast.

COWARDLY = Wanting courage to face danger; timid; timorous; fearful; Proceeding from fear of danger; as cowardly silence.

UNSETTLED = Unfixed; unhinged; rendered fluctuating. Lacking stability; Not yet resolved.

PEACE = A state of quiet or tranquility; freedom from disturbance or agitation.

BEQUEATH = To give or leave by will; to- devise some species of property by testament; pass (something) on or leave (something) to someone else.

PERMIT = To allow; to grant leave or liberty to by express consent.

PERFECT = Finished; complete; consummate; not defective; having all that is requisite to its nature and kind; Complete in moral excellencies; Manifesting perfection.

CONFIDENCE = A trusting, or reliance; an assurance of mind or firm belief in the integrity, stability or veracity of another, or in the truth and reality of a fact.

TRIBULATION = Severe affliction; distresses of life; vexations. A state of great trouble or suffering.

TRIAL = Experience; suffering that puts strength, patience or faith to the test; afflictions or temptations that exercise and prove the graces or virtues of men.

DISTRESS = Extreme pain; anguish of body or mind; as, to suffer great distress from the gout, or from the loss of near friends; Affliction; calamity; misery; A state of danger.

FRUSTRATION = The act of frustrating; disappointment; defeat; The feeling of being upset or annoyed, especially because of the inability to change or achieve something.

COURAGE = Bravery; intrepidity; that quality of mind which enables men to encounter danger and difficulties with firmness, or without fear or depression of spirits; valor; boldness; resolution.

CONFIDENT = One entrusted with secrets; a confidential or bosom friend.

CERTAIN = Sure; true; undoubted; unquestionable; that cannot be denied; existing in fact and truth.

UNDAUNTED = Not daunted; not subdued or depressed by fear; intrepid; Not intimidated or discouraged by difficulty, danger, or disappointment

OVERCOME = To gain superiority; to be victorious; To conquer; to vanquish. To subdue; as, to overcome enemies in battle.

DEPRIVED = Bereft; divested; hindered; stripped of office or dignity; deposed; degraded.

POWER = the faculty of doing or performing anything; the faculty of moving or of producing a change in something; ability or strength; the capacity or ability to direct or influence the behavior of others or the course of events.

HARM = Injury; hurt; damage; detriment; physical injury, especially that which is deliberately inflicted.

CONQUERED = Overcome; subdued; vanquished; gained; won.

IDLY = To refrain from acting or intervening while something bad happens or unfolds.

VINDICATION = The defense of anything, or a justification against denial or censure, or against objections or accusations. The action of clearing someone of blame or suspicion.

EXPERIENCE = To know by practice or trial; to gain knowledge or skill by practice or by a series of observations. Practical contact with and observation of facts or events.

LET'S PRAY

Father in the Name of Jesus we want to praise and worship you, for you are the ONE AND TRUE & LIVING GOD!

We want to thank you for allowing us to gather together to celebrate the FREEDOM that YOU have given unto us.

We ask that you grant us true peace and wisdom as we stand and fight for our FREEDOM in the realm of the spirit, as well as with boots on the ground.

You said in your HOLY WORD, that we are not wrestling with flesh and blood, but against the master spirits who are the world rulers of this present darkness, and against the spirit forces of wickedness in the heavenly places.

Therefore, we put on your complete armor, so that we may be able to RESIST and STAND our ground during this EVIL day of DANGER.

We apply the BLOOD OF JESUS over each and every one of us as we put on your complete armor.

We thank you for Your ARMOUR (Ephesians 6:10-17), which is:

1. **THE BELT OF TRUTH**, which is your word, and your word is the antidote against the lies of the enemy.

2. **THE BREASTPLATE RIGHTEOUS,** which is to repent and be forgiven for our sins and to do what is right.

3. **THE SHOES OF THE GOSPEL OF PEACE,** which is to stand ready and firm to combat the enemy.

4. **THE SHIELD OF FAITH,** which quenches and puts out ALL the fiery darts and strategies of the evil hidden enemies.

5. **THE HELMET OF SALVATION,** which protects our mind from the discouragements, anxieties, depression, fear, and despair in the world today.

6. **THE SWORD OF THE SPIRIT,** which is the living and powerful word of God. The Word of God is sharper than any two-edged sword.

So, Father, we use TODAY and EVERYDAY, every piece of your Armor to RESIST and DEFEAT all the STRATEGIES, all the PLOTS, all the SCHEMES, and all the PLANS of the evil enemies that have come against our Nation, our President Donald J. Trump, and our State.

We say that when this WAR is all over, we will still be standing up STRONGER and with TOTAL VICTORY IN EVERY AREA.

In Jesus' Name we pray, AMEN!!

INVOCATION FOR THE NATION

By Bernadette Smith

Father, in the name of Jesus, we come before You, thanking and praising You for who You are and for what You are going to do on behalf of our great country.

We feel and see the natural. That darkness is trying to take over our country.

But we understand that the real battle is the battle between good and evil, a battle between the light and the darkness.

We are up against demonic forces that have been controlling our nation for too long. For we are not wrestling against flesh and blood, but against evil wicked spirits, against the master spirits who are the world rulers of this present darkness.

Heavenly Father, You have given to us the tools and the strategies to fight with.

We must Fight in the spirit as well as with BOOTS on the GROUND; But we must first fight in the realm of the SPIRIT by putting on our COMPLETE ARMOR, so that we may be able to RESIST and STAND our ground during this evil day of danger.

We thank you for your ARMOR, which is:

1. THE BELT OF TRUTH, which is Your word, and Your word is the antidote against the lies of the enemy.

2. THE BREASTPLATE OF RIGHTEOUSNESS, which is to repent and be forgiven for our sins and to do what is right.

3. THE SHOES OF THE GOSPEL OF PEACE, which is to stand ready and firm to combat the enemy.

349

4. THE SHIELD OF FAITH, which quenches and puts out ALL the fiery darts and strategies of the hidden evil enemies.

5. THE HELMET OF SALVATION, which protects our mind from discouragements, anxieties, depression, fear, and despair in our world today.

6. THE SWORD OF THE SPIRIT, which is the living and powerful word of God. The Word of God is sharper than any two-edged sword.

So, Father, we use TODAY and EVERYDAY, every piece of Your armor to RESIST and DEFEAT all the STRATEGIES, all the PLOTS, all the SCHEMES, and all the PLANS of the evil enemies that have come against our country.

There will be a great reset, but the great reset will be us taking back our country; And WE MUST take it back NOW!!

It is high time and VITAL that we FOCUS on what UNITES us and RISE above what divides us.

So, we now take our AUTHORITY in the name of Jesus, and **we decree and declare** that our country is back to its Judeo Christian values.

We decree and declare that we are ending the war on our babies and our children.

We decree and declare that we are enforcing our United States Constitution.

We decree and declare that a mighty revival is sweeping throughout our land.

We decree and declare that when this WAR is all over, we will still be standing up STRONGER and with TOTAL VICTORY in every area.

We decree and declare that we are once again that SHINING COUNTRY that sits on a hill for all the WORLD to see.

This we pray in the name of Jesus Christ, Amen!!

THE LORD IS OUR SHEPHERD

he Lord is our Shepherd (to FEED, GUIDE and SHIELD us), we shall not lack for anything. He makes us lie down in fresh tender green pastures. He leads us beside the still and restful waters. He RESTORES our SOUL. He leads us in the path of righteousness for HIS NAME's sake. Though we may walk through the valley of the SHADOW of death, we do not have to fear any evil; for God is with us. His rod and his staff, comfort us. He prepares a table before us in the presence of our enemies; He anoints our head with oil and our cup runs over. His total GOODNESS and His total MERCIES shall follow us ALL the days of our lives, And we shall DWELL in the house of the Lord FOREVER!! (Psalms 23)

Some of you may be going through dark times in your lives personally. Our country is seemingly going through dark times as well. It may seem like we are experiencing the valley of the shadow of death.

Remember: it is ONLY a shadow.

Our God is with you, and He is with our country. When God is with us, we do not have to fear ANY EVIL. When God is with us PROTECTION and PEACE is available to us. Let us continue to rest in His strength and ability to bring us to TOTAL VICTORY!!!

Remember our job is to follow and obey Him and His job is to perform!! He for sure will perform BIGGLY on your behalf and upon our country!!

He is preparing a great big bowl of VICTORY at the table for ALL of us!!

I want to encourage ALL who have not made Jesus Lord over your lives, to turn to the back of this book and pray the simple prayer of salvation I have provided for you to pray right now. This is our security for eternal life and it is truly an amazing, exciting, and peaceful journey.

Love you ALL to life!

DEFINITIONS:

SHEPHERD = One who leads, protects, and governs their people, and provides for their welfare.

FEED = To supply with provisions.

GUIDE = A person who leads or directs another in his way or course of life.

SHIELD = To cover from danger, to defend, to protect, to secure from assault or injury, to cover as with a shield.

RESTORE = To bring back; Reinstate; Return to a former condition, place, or position; to repair.

SOUL = Your mind; Your Will and your emotions

MERCY = Compassion or forgiveness shown towards someone who it is within one's power to punish or harm.

GOODNESS = Kindness, Benevolence of nature; Mercy

DWELL = To abide as a permanent resident, or to inhabit for a time; to live in a place.

FOREVER = For all future time; for always; continually.

PROTECTION = The act of protecting; defense; sheltering from evil, preservation from loss, injury, or annoyance.

PEACE = A state of quiet or tranquility; freedom from disturbance or agitation.

PRAYER FOR SALVATION

Jesus is returning soon. Do you know where you will spend eternity? If you are not sure, you can be sure today by asking Him to come into your heart. Pray this prayer from your heart and you can be assured that you will spend eternity in Heaven with Jesus.

> *Dear Heavenly Father, I come to you in the Name of Jesus. In John 6:37 Your word says: He that cometh to you, you will in NO WISE cast out. In Romans 10:13 it states: whosoever shall call upon the name of the Lord, shall be saved. I am calling on your name therefore I am saved.*

You also said, *"If thou shalt confess with thy mouth the Lord Jesus, and shalt believe in thine heart that God Hath raised him from the dead, thou shalt be saved. For with the heart man believeth unto righteousness; and with the mouth confession is made unto salvation"* (Romans 10:9-10). I believe in my heart Jesus Christ is the Son of God.

I believe that He was raised from the dead for my justification, and I confess Him now as my Lord. Because Your Word says, *"With the heart man believeth unto righteousness,"* and I do believe with my heart, I have now become the righteousness of God in Christ (2 Corinthians 5:21)... AND I AM SAVED! THANK YOU, LORD!

PRAYER FOR BAPTISM OF THE HOLY SPIRIT

Baptism in the Holy Spirit and fire is a gift from God as promised by the Lord Jesus Christ to all believers in this dispensation and is received after the new birth. This experience is accompanied by the initial evidence of speaking in other tongues as the Holy Spirit Himself gives utterance (Matt. 3:11; John 14:16,17; Acts 1:8; Acts 2:38,39; Acts 19:1–7; Acts 2:1–4).

Baptism in the Holy Spirit is a gift from God as promised by the Lord Jesus Christ to all believers in this dispensation and is received subsequent to the new birth. This experience is accompanied by the initial evidence of speaking in other tongues as the Holy Spirit Himself gives utterance (Matt. 3:11; John 14:16,17; Acts 1:8; Acts 2:38,39; Acts 19:1–7; Acts 2:1–4).

If you would like to receive the Baptism of the Holy Ghost pray this prayer with me:

Father God you said in your Holy Word, that if we then being evil know how to give good gifts. HOW MUCH MORE shall you give the Holy Spirit to me and anyone that asks? (Luke 11:13)

I am asking that you fill me with the Holy Spirit. The Holy Spirit rises up BIGLY within me as I praise You. Give me the utterance Father, and I fully expect to speak in tongues.

A LITTLE ABOUT THE AUTHOR:

I hear so often, "Bernadette how do you do what you do?", "How do you hear from the Lord?" "How do you know what you know?", etc.

I am reminded of my youth:

As a young girl I would play with Jesus. I would tell my mom "Mommy I played with Jesus last night!" I would tell her this from time to time. One day she asked me, "Bernadette what does Jesus look like"? I said He was a (little) white ball. As I grew up, I realized that I was playing in Glory.

As I experienced the Glory and developed my relationship with the Lord, I would see and hear about things to come:

In September 2001 I had a dream. In this dream, I saw three Eagles blow up and explode in midair. It was a massive explosion. The dream was so real. I wondered what this could mean. I called my mom and said, "Mommy, have you ever heard of eagles blowing up in midair?" She said no and wondered also what this dream could mean. I prayed about it, but not fervently. About two weeks later, I heard on the news, while in my car, that 3 American Airlines exploded! Two crashed into the twin towers in NYC and one into the Pentagon. (9/11/01) When I got home and looked at the news, it looked just like the dream that I had just two weeks before. The Lord was showing me what Satan had planned against our country. I did struggle a bit asking myself why I had not fervently prayed into that dream.

I had this dream around 10 years before COVID struck the world:

I was in the hospital sitting up in the hospital bed and a doctor and a nurse walked up to me. the Dr. had a needle in his hand getting ready to give me a shot, I spoke up and said, "What are you doing? I do not need a shot." He and the nurse proceeded to force me down on the bed and forced the shot into my arm. They walked away and I looked up towards Heaven with my hands in the air and said, "NOW WHAT GOD?" He said to me neutralize it. He said to neutralize it with my blood (the blood of Jesus). When something is neutralized, it DESTROYS and renders something INEFFECTIVE or HARMLESS by an opposite and DIFFERENT force or effect. The DIFFERENT substance in this case is the Blood of Jesus. Jesus went to the cross and shed His precious blood for our healing. He paid the price and destroyed sickness and disease at the cross of Calvary. All we need to do is have Faith in His work at Calvary and receive our healing.

On February 3rd, 2016:

I was praying in the Holy Spirit for about 3 hours. The Lord began to speak to me and say, "Things are coming on the face of the earth". He said it 3 times. I then said Lord, what things? He said to me, "Chaos", and then He said, "and great things." I then began to say, "I thank you Lord for protecting us from the chaos that's coming on the face of the earth, and I thank you for preparing us to receive the great things that are coming on the face of the earth."

He then spoke up and said to me "Rise up and declare to this generation time is short, get your house in order (your soul =mind, Will and emotion- the real you). The Lord is at hand, prepare to meet Him. He then spoke again to me and said "Darkness shall cover the earth, great darkness; But the earth shall be filled with my glory" (Habakkuk 2:14)

On April 23, 2021:

I woke up asking God again, Lord I said, "what's coming on the face of the earth?", I heard "Darkness and gross darkness, but I will save my people." He went on to say, "I will rescue my people." He said to me, "stay in the light as He "Jesus" is the light!! Stay in Jesus!!!"

360

In 2018:

I had a dream that President Trump was holding a rally outside of an airport. At this time, he was only holding rallies inside of venues. Outside, the airport was packed with people. After the President's speech, he got into a green helicopter. As the helicopter was going up, I heard these words come from the men inside the helicopter, "we got him now". My heart began to sink. I started praying and alerting people to pray for our President! A year or so later, because of Covid, President Trump began to hold rallies outside. He held an outdoor rally in Washington Michigan where I attended. That rally looked identical to the one in my dream a year or so before.

Miracles:

In my prayer time with the Lord l, I would often pray, "Lord, I thank you for using me to set the captives free, to heal the sick, to raise the dead, and to open up the blinded eyes." One day I was ministering at a conference. I called up people who wanted prayer. The altar was filled with people. My husband came up to help me pray. As I was going down the line and setting the captives free, I came across a blind young lady that was blind from birth. Immediately I heard the Lord say to me, "Are you ready?" I knew exactly what He was talking about. I then looked at the blind young lady and said, "I came here for you". I proceeded along with my husband to lay hands on her eyes and command blindness to leave her. She was immediately made whole. I said to her, "Follow me," I began to walk around the front of the church, and she followed me. She said to me, "I once was blind, but now I see." She was 21 years old.

In another meeting, as I was praying for people I came across a lady, who lost her speech due to a brain surgery. She came up for prayer and I prayed the prayer of faith over her, and she immediately started speaking. In that same meeting, there were three beautiful model-looking young ladies that came up for prayer. As I laid my hands on the first one, I noticed that there was a demon inside of her. I proceeded to cast out that devil, the young lady fell to the ground and began to move like a snake. I continue to speak to that demon and command it to go. The demon left and the young lady was set free. Well as I prayed for the 2nd and 3rd young ladies, the same thing happened. Those 3 beautiful young ladies got totally free from the bondage of demons! Glory to God!

I am looking forward to expounding upon these testimonies and sharing many more miracles that I have experienced in my life in my coming books.

ALL OF THE GLORY GOES TO GOD!!

Other Awards and Accolades

- **CITIZENS LIBERATING MICHIGAN AWARD**
- **COURAGE UNDER FIRE AWARD**